高等学校本科英语教改新教材　　　　　　　　总 主 编　史宝辉

中国当代社会与文化英文教程

（第三版）

主　编　訾　缨　李　芝
副主编　白雪莲　常　青
编　者　（按拼音顺序排列）
　　　　姜　佳　龙　莺　卢晓敏　罗凌志
　　　　南宫梅芳　彭北萍　王雪梅　武田田
　　　　杨慧媛　张永萍

北京大学出版社
PEKING UNIVERSITY PRESS

图书在版编目(CIP)数据

中国当代社会与文化英文教程 / 訾缨，李芝主编 . —3 版 . —北京：北京大学出版社，2023.1
高等学校本科英语教改新教材
ISBN 978-7-301-33522-2

Ⅰ.①中⋯ Ⅱ.①訾⋯ ②李⋯ Ⅲ.①英语–高等学校–教材 Ⅳ.①H319.39

中国版本图书馆 CIP 数据核字（2022）第 197571 号

书　　　名	中国当代社会与文化英文教程（第三版）
	ZHONGGUO DANGDAI SHEHUI YU WENHUA YINGWEN JIAOCHENG (DI-SAN BAN)
著作责任者	訾　缨　李　芝　主编
责任编辑	李　颖
标准书号	ISBN 978-7-301-33522-2
出版发行	北京大学出版社
地　　　址	北京市海淀区成府路 205 号　100871
网　　　址	http://www.pup.cn　新浪微博：@北京大学出版社
电子邮箱	编辑部 pupwaiwen@pup.cn　总编室 zpup@pup.cn
电　　　话	邮购部 010-62752015　发行部 010-62750672　编辑部 010-62754382
印刷者	河北博文科技印务有限公司
经销者	新华书店
	787 毫米 ×1092 毫米　16 开本　11.25 印张　392 千字
	2013 年 3 月第 1 版　2015 年 1 月第 2 版
	2023 年 1 月第 3 版　2025 年 1 月第 2 次印刷
定　　　价	55.00 元

未经许可，不得以任何方式复制或抄袭本书之部分或全部内容。
版权所有，侵权必究
举报电话：010-62752024　电子邮箱：fd@pup.cn
图书如有印装质量问题，请与出版部联系，电话：010-62756370

第三版前言

由北京市教学名师史宝辉教授担任总主编的"高等学校本科英语教改新教材"已列入北京大学出版社的出版规划。目前修订再版的教材为《中国当代社会与文化英文教程（第三版）》。这是以英语为媒介传播和弘扬中华文化的高等院校文化素质类通识课教材，旨在通过对中国当代社会历史文化等方面的介绍以及相关英语表达方式的训练，引导青年学子领悟中华文化精髓，涵养人文精神，培植文化自信和文化自觉，增强文化传承的使命感和民族自豪感，提高"讲好中国故事"的能力，为"中华文化走出去"做好必要的人才储备和积累。

《中国当代社会与文化英文教程（第三版）》是2015年版的修订版。在教材修订中，我们始终坚持立德树人、培根铸魂、启智增慧的正确方向，注重与弘扬中华文化的课程思政深度融合，力求使学生通过语言学习、知识获取和文化认知，树立正确的世界观、人生观和价值观。该教材以知识素养能力培养一体化原则为指导，以培养学生语言输出能力为重点，按照"双一流"和"新文科"建设背景下的人才培养要求，以中国当代社会文化内容为依托，教授学生在语言输出实践中如何使用流畅、得体的英语将中国当代社会、政治、经济、教育、文化领域的话题进行话语构建和表达，实现语言和文化两个层面的输出，从而完成大学英语从语言技能教学向文化教学的转变，推进中华文化的传播。

《中国当代社会与文化英文教程（第三版）》提供了一种图文并茂地展现中国当代社会历史文化风貌的方式，凸显重要主题。全书共分为10个单元，每个单元以一个主题为中心，从中国国家基本概况谈起，涵盖各族人民、语言文学、教育制度、科学技术、传统节日、壮丽山河、饮食文化、中医疗法、中华瑰宝等诸多方面的文化知识。通过听、说、读、写、译等多种训练方式强化学生对中华文化的了解和领悟。课程内容生动、直观，符合当代大学生的认知心理。教材语篇长度、难度适中，备有词汇表、文化背景知识脚注，每篇文章后均有长难句翻译，方便学习者学习和查找。

第三版对语言文学、教育制度、科学技术三个单元的选篇做了较大幅度的修改，更新了课文内容和统计数据，去除了内容相对陈旧的篇章，增加了与时俱进的选篇和经典作品及人物的介绍，比如疫情时期的在线教育，科幻小说与电影，问鼎茅盾文学奖的长篇小说《白鹿原》及其作者陈忠实，"捧着一颗心来，不带半根草去"的中国人民教育家、思想家陶行知等。

各单元根据话题设计的教学环节和练习形式更加多样，练习以提高"写"和"说"的能力为突破口，设计分为三个层次：第一个层次注重语言和内容的基础理解，第二个层次关注学生的思辨能力发展，第三个层次侧重语言输出能力的培养。特别增加了汉译英和段落匹配等练习形式，以期对学生通过四、六级考试有所帮助。与教材配套的课堂版教学电子课件，制作精美，信息量大，含有大量与单元主题相关的精美图片和音视频资料，使用便捷，有助于教师备课、授课和学生拓展学习。

《中国当代社会与文化英文教程（第三版）》读者群广泛，适用性强，主要读者对象为高等院校本科生，亦可供在华各国留学生使用。

本教材是"高等学校本科英语教改新教材"系列之一，是教育部新文科研究与改革实践项目"产出导向与持续质量改进模式下的新文科外语类课程体系和教材体系建设与实践研究"的阶段性成果，得到了教育部"双万计划"一流本科专业建设项目、北京市与在京高校共建项目、中央高校基本科研业务费专项资金和北京林业大学教务处（"多层次模块化链条式大学英语人才培养课程体系建设"）的支持和资助。

由于本次修订更新和增加了大量内容，任务量大，难免出现这样或那样的问题和疏漏，欢迎广大教师、学生和使用者提出宝贵意见，以便我们及时做出修改。

编者
2022年10月

中国当代社会与文化英文教程（第三版）

尊敬的老师：

您好！

为了方便您更好地使用本教材，获得最佳教学效果，我们特向使用该书作为教材的教师赠送本教材配套参考资料。如有需要，请完整填写"教师联系表"并加盖所在单位系（院）公章，免费向出版社索取。

北京大学出版社

教 师 联 系 表

教材名称	中国当代社会与文化英文教程（第三版）					
姓名：		性别：		职务：		职称：
E-mail：			联系电话：		邮政编码：	
供职学校：			所在院系：			（章）
学校地址：						
教学科目与年级：			班级人数：			
通信地址：						

填写完毕后，请将此表邮寄给我们，我们将为您免费寄送本教材配套资料，谢谢！

北京市海淀区成府路 205 号
北京大学出版社外语编辑部　李　颖　　　　邮购部电话：010-62752015
邮政编码：100871　　　　　　　　　　　　市场营销部电话：010-62750672
电子邮箱：evalee1770@sina.com　　　　　　外语编辑部电话：010-62754382

目 录

Unit 1　Talking About China ·············· 1
　Section A　Reading and Writing ·············· 1
　　Text 1　General Survey ·············· 1
　　Text 2　Geographic Overview ·············· 3
　Section B　Listening and Speaking ·············· 7
　　Text 3　Situational Dialogue: Chinese History ·············· 7
　　Text 4　Cities to See in China ·············· 10
Unit 2　Chinese People ·············· 18
　Section A　Reading and Writing ·············· 18
　　Text 1　Han People ·············· 18
　　Text 2　A Glimpse of Chinese 55 Ethnic Minorities ·············· 20
　Section B　Listening and Speaking ·············· 25
　　Text 3　Situational Dialogue: Modern Chinese Youth ·············· 25
　　Text 4　Mosuo People—A Matriarchal Society ·············· 27
Unit 3　Chinese Language and Literature ·············· 36
　Section A　Reading and Writing ·············· 36
　　Text 1　Jin Yong, a Literary Swordsman ·············· 36
　　Text 2　White Deer Plain ·············· 38
　Section B　Listening and Speaking ·············· 42
　　Text 3　Situational Dialogue: An Interview of Liu Cixin ·············· 42
　　Text 4　A Talk on Chinese Literature in the 20th Century ·············· 44
Unit 4　Chinese Education ·············· 52
　Section A　Reading and Writing ·············· 52
　　Text 1　Reforming Chinese Education ·············· 52
　　Text 2　Online Education: Ushering in a New Era of China's Education ·············· 54
　Section B　Listening and Speaking ·············· 58
　　Text 3　Situational Dialogue: China's Education ·············· 58
　　Text 4　Tao Xingzhi ·············· 60
Unit 5　Economy, Science and Technology ·············· 71
　Section A　Reading and Writing ·············· 71
　　Text 1　A New Legend for an Ancient City ·············· 71

	Text 2	China Is Pushing Ahead in New Fronts of Science and Technology Development ··· 73
	Section B	Listening and Speaking ··· 79
	Text 3	Situational Dialogue: China's Manned Submersible ························· 79
	Text 4	A Tour Guide Commentary on Qinghai-Tibet Railway ····················· 81

Unit 6   Chinese Holidays and Folk Customs ·· 89
    Section A   Reading and Writing ·· 89
        Text 1   Chinese New Year in the Modern World: A Traditional Chinese Holiday Today ··· 89
        Text 2   The Dragon Boat Festival ·· 91
    Section B   Listening and Speaking ·· 95
        Text 3   Situational Dialogue: Our Traditional Holidays—Still Meaningful? ··············· 95
        Text 4   A Speech on Double Seventh Festival ··· 97

Unit 7   Land of Splendor ·· 107
    Section A   Reading and Writing ·· 107
        Text 1   The Yellow River ·· 107
        Text 2   The Great Wall ·· 110
    Section B   Listening and Speaking ·· 113
        Text 3   Situational Dialogue: The Summer Palace ·· 113
        Text 4   Sacred Mountains of China: Four Great Mountains of Buddhism ············· 115

Unit 8   Chinese Food Culture ·· 124
    Section A   Reading and Writing ·· 124
        Text 1   The Principles of Chinese Cuisine ·· 124
        Text 2   Regional Cuisines ·· 126
    Section B   Listening and Speaking ·· 130
        Text 3   Situational Dialogue: Beijing Roast Duck ·· 130
        Text 4   A Tour Guide Commentary on Beijing Snacks ································ 132

Unit 9   Chinese Medicine ·· 140
    Section A   Reading and Writing ·· 140
        Text 1   An Introduction to Traditional Chinese Medicine ···························· 140
        Text 2   An Introduction to Acupuncture ··· 143
    Section B   Listening and Speaking ·· 147
        Text 3   Situational Dialogue: About Qi-gong Therapy ································· 147
        Text 4   A Lecture on Beijing Tongrentang ··· 148

Unit 10 National Treasures ··· 156
    Section A   Reading and Writing ·· 156
        Text 1   Wushu and Tai Ji Quan ·· 156
        Text 2   Chinese Handicrafts ··· 158
    Section B   Listening and Speaking ·· 161
        Text 3   Situational Dialogue: Beijing Opera ··· 161
        Text 4   A Tour Guide Commentary on Dashilar ·· 163

Unit 1 Talking About China

导读

本单元旨在通过对中国国家标志、地理特征、历史朝代和主要城市的介绍，使学生能运用相关的英语表达进行跨文化交流，让世界了解中国。

Before You Start

While you are preparing for this unit, think about the following questions:
1. What national symbols do you think of at the sight of the word "China"?
2. What are the geographic features of your hometown?
3. Can you list the dynasties in Chinese history chronologically?

Section A Reading and Writing

Text 1 General Survey

Country Name

Contemporary China's official name is the People's Republic of China, often abbreviated as P. R. China or PRC. China is called *Zhōngguó* in Mandarin Chinese. The first character *Zhōng* (中) means "central" or "middle", while *guó* (国) means "state" or "nation." Many Western works use the translation "middle kingdom" or "central kingdom." In ancient texts, *Zhōngguó* referred to a state, a city or the group of states in the central plain.

National Flag

The national flag of China is red with one large yellow five-pointed star and four smaller ones (arranged in a vertical arc toward the middle star) in the upper hoist-side corner. The color of red symbolizes the spirit of revolution, and the five stars signify the unity of the people of China under the leadership of the Communist Party of China (CPC). The flag was officially unveiled in Beijing's Tian'anmen Square on October 1, 1949, the formal announcement of the founding of the People's Republic of China.

National Emblem

① The design of the national emblem of the People's Republic of China, published by the Central People's Government on September 20, 1950, shows Tian'anmen under the light of five stars, and it is framed with ears of grain and a cogwheel. Tian'anmen is the place where the inauguration of the People's Republic of China was held. The cogwheel and the ears of grain represent the working class and the peasantry respectively. The five stars symbolize the solidarity of the various nationalities of China. The emblem clearly indicates that the People's Republic of China is a socialist state led by the working class and based on the alliance of industrial and agricultural workers.

National Anthem

"March of the Volunteers," written in 1935, with lyrics by the poet Tian Han and music by the composer Nie Er, honors those who went to the front to fight against the Japanese invaders in northeast China in the 1930s.

Lyrics (reference translation)

March of the Volunteers

Arise, ye who refuse to be slaves!
Let us amount our flesh and blood towards our new Great Wall!
The Chinese nation faces its greatest peril,
The thundering roar of our peoples will be heard!
Arise! Arise! Arise!
We are many, but our hearts beat as one!
Selflessly braving the enemy's gunfire, march on!
Selflessly braving the enemy's gunfire, march on!
March on! March on! On!

Administrative Divisions & Capital

The entire country is divided into 23 provinces, five autonomous regions (Tibet, Xinjiang, Inner Mongolia, Guangxi and Ningxia), four municipalities (Beijing, Shanghai, Tianjin and Chongqing) and two special administrative regions (Hong Kong and Macau).

Beijing is the capital of the People's Republic of China. It is not only the nation's political center, but also its cultural, scientific and educational center, and a key transportation hub.

People

China, as the world's most populous nation, has a population of over 1.41 billion (2020). Out of every five persons living in this world, one is a Chinese. People live mainly around the coastal areas and industrialized zones of central China.

China is home to 56 ethnic peoples. The Han people account for about 91 percent of the total population (2020), while the other 55 ethnic groups are known as minorities. All ethnic groups in China are equal according to the law. The state protects their lawful rights and interests and promotes equality, unity, and mutual help among them.

Language

The official language of China is standard Chinese or Mandarin, known as Putonghua. It is based on the Beijing dialect, but its vocabulary is drawn from the northern dialects. Many other dialects and ethnic minority languages are also spoken.

All of the Chinese dialects share a common written form that has evolved and been standardized during two millennia and serves as a unifying bond among the Chinese people. The government has aggressively developed both simplified Chinese and Pinyin (phonetic spelling) as ways to increase literacy and transliterate Chinese names.

National Animal

The Giant Panda is regarded as a national treasure. Just over 1,000 survive in the wild and most of them live in Sichuan province. The panda has a black-and-white coat. ② It is easily recognized by its large, distinctive black patches around the eyes, over the ears, and across its round body. Though it belongs to the order Carnivora (食肉类), the panda has a diet which is 99% bamboo. (733 words)

Difficult Sentences

① The design of the national emblem of the People's Republic of China, published by the Central People's Government on September 20, 1950, shows Tian'anmen under the light of five stars, and it is framed with ears of grain and a cogwheel.
中华人民共和国国徽的设计由中央人民政府于1950年9月20日颁布，图案中间是五星照耀下的天安门，周围是谷穗和齿轮。

② It is easily recognized by its large, distinctive black patches around the eyes, over the ears, and across its round body.
熊猫的眼睛周围、耳朵上、滚圆的身体上都长着大块的标志性的黑色皮毛，很容易识别。

Text 2 Geographic Overview

China, an ancient, mysterious and beautiful land, is located in the eastern part of the Asian continent, on the western Pacific Rim. It is a vast land, covering 9.6 million square kilometers. China is approximately seventeen times the size of France, 1 million square kilometers smaller than all of Europe, and 600,000 square kilometers smaller than Oceania (Australia, New Zealand, and the islands of the south and central Pacific). Additional offshore territory, including territorial waters, special economic areas, and the continental shelf, totals over 3 million square kilometers, bringing China's overall territory to almost 13 million square kilometers. When inhabitants of eastern China are greeting the dawn, people in western China still face four more hours of darkness. When northern China is still gripped in a world of ice and snow, flowers are already blooming in the warm and pleasant south. China possesses 20,000 kilometers of land border, plus 18,000 kilometers of coastline.

Broadly speaking, the relief of China is high in the west and low in the east; consequently, the direction of flow of the major rivers is generally eastward. The surface may be divided into three steps, or levels.

① The first step is represented by the Plateau of Tibet, which is located in both the Tibet autonomous region and the province of Qinghai and which, with an average elevation of well over 4,000 meters (13,000 feet) above sea level, is the loftiest highland area in the world and often known as "the roof of the world." At the southern rim of the Tibetan Plateau, on the Nepalese-Tibetan border, are the soaring Himalayan Mountains. Here stands the world's tallest peak, Mount Qomolangma (meaning "Goddess" in Tibetan), which is 8848.86 (2020) meters (29,032 feet) high.

The second step lies to the north of the Kunlun and Qilian mountains and (farther south) to the east of the Qionglai and Daliang ranges. ② There the mountains descend sharply to heights of between 1,800 and 900 meters (6,000 and 3,000 feet), after which basins intermingle with plateaus. This step includes the Mongolian Plateau, the Tarim Basin, the Loess Plateau (loess is a yellow-gray dust deposited by the wind), the Sichuan Basin, and the Yunnan-Guizhou (Yungui) Plateau.

The third step stretches down to the Pacific Ocean and is the most fertile and populous area of China. Almost all of this area is made up of hills and plains lying below 450 meters (1,500 feet). In the far north, the terrain is low and flat, broken only occasionally by mountains. Farther south are the vast flood plains of China's great rivers. In the far south, there are hills crossed by river valleys.

The most remarkable feature of China's relief is the vast extent of mountain chains. By rough estimate, about one-third of the total area of China consists of mountains. China has some of the world's tallest mountains and the highest and largest plateau, in addition to extensive coastal plains. The five major landforms—mountain, plateau, hill, plain, and basin—are all well represented. China's complex natural environment and rich natural resources are closely connected with the varied nature of its relief.

③ China's climate diversity mirrors that of its topography, ranging from extremely dry desert-like conditions in the northwest to a tropical monsoon climate in the southeast. From September to April of the following year, dry and cold air masses blow from Siberia and the Mongolian Plateau, resulting in cold and dry winters, and great differences between the temperatures of north and south China. From April to September, warm and humid summer monsoons blow from the seas in the east and south, resulting in overall high temperatures and abundant rainfall, and the range of temperatures between north and south is quite small. (621words)

(Based on: *http://english.www.gov.cn/archive/china_abc/2014/09/02/content_281474985266381.htm* 2022年5月9日访问)

Difficult Sentences

① The first step is represented by the Plateau of Tibet, which is located in both the Tibet autonomous region and the province of Qinghai and which, with an average elevation of well over 4,000 meters (13,000 feet) above sea level, is the loftiest highland area in the world and often known as the "roof of the world."
第一阶梯以青藏高原为主,青藏高原位于西藏自治区和青海省境内,平均海拔在4,000米(13,000英尺)以上,是世界上最高的高原,有"世界屋脊"之称。

② There the mountains descend sharply to heights of between 1,800 and 900 meters (6,000 and 3,000 feet), after which basins intermingle with plateaus.
那里的山脉海拔高度迅速下降到1,800米至900米(6,000英尺至3,000英尺),接下来盆地和高原交错分布。

③ China's climate diversity mirrors that of its topography, ranging from extremely dry desert-like conditions in the northwest to a tropical monsoon climate in the southeast.
中国的气候与地形一样多样,既有西北部极度干旱的沙漠性气候,又有东南部热带季风性气候。

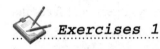 Exercises 1

Task 1 Short Answer Questions
Directions: *Read Text 1 and Text 2 and then answer the following questions briefly.*
1. What is the title of the national anthem of P. R. China?
2. How many administrative divisions are there in P. R. China?
3. Where is China located?
4. Why do major rivers in China generally flow from west to east?
5. What is the world's loftiest highland?

Task 2 Reading Comprehension

Part A

Directions: *In this section, there are 5 incomplete sentences. You are required to select one word for each blank from a list of choices given in the word bank below. You may not use any of the words in the bank more than once.*

| hoist | relief | millennia | unveiled | lofty |
| gripped | plain | inauguration | monsoon | deposits |

1. As the river slows down, it _____ a layer of soil.

2. The _____ tower of the City Hall overlooked the whole panorama of the streets and avenues.

3. The city _____ a package of measures to deal with the threat.

4. In his _____ speech, the newly elected president promised to fight corruption and promote social justice.

5. Every summer, tourists flock to the _____ for its abundant wildlife and spectacular scenery.

Part B

Directions: *In this section, you are going to read a passage with five statements attached to it. Each statement contains information given in one of the paragraphs. Identify the paragraph from which the information is derived. Each paragraph is marked with a letter.*

A) The vast landmass of China lies in Asia, the world's largest continent, and faces the Pacific, the world's largest ocean, along an extensive shoreline. The country's climate is thus heavily influenced by the seasonal movement of the tropical Pacific air mass and the continental Siberian air mass.

B) The Siberian air mass is extremely cold and dry. Because North China is affected by this air mass most of the time, it is dry with clear weather and an abundance of sunshine during the winter months.

C) As the Siberian air mass spreads southward, the Qinling Mountains become an effective barrier to the advance of the cold waves. Thus, the Huai River-Qinling Mountains line is generally regarded as the geographical dividing line between North China and South China. South of the line, the mean January temperature increases progressively, rising from freezing to 22°C on the southern coast of the Hainan Island. Snow rarely falls and the rivers do not freeze. North of this line, the temperature drops from freezing to –28°C in the northern part of Heilongjiang.

D) In summer when the tropical Pacific air mass predominates, the frontal zone between the two air masses shifts northward; as a result, North China receives heavier rainfall. When the southeastern monsoon slackens, however, the frontal zone moves southward, and central China receives more rainfall, which can cause flooding.

E) As the Pacific monsoon gradually loses its moisture on the way to the north, precipitation in China decreases from the southeast to the northwest. Northwest of a line linking the Greater

Khingan, Yin, Lang, Qilian, and Altun ranges, the annual precipitation is less than 10 inches (25 cm). Because these regions are far from the sea, high mountains prevent the southern monsoon from reaching them, and only grasslands are found there. In western Inner Mongolia, the Gansu Corridor, and the Tarim Basin, the annual precipitation drops to 4 inches (10 cm) or less. These are areas of true desert, where sometimes not a single drop of moisture is received for several years.

( ) 1. The northern parts generally receive less rainfall than the southern ones annually.
( ) 2. The tropical Pacific air mass is the chief source of summer rainfall.
( ) 3. It is dry in the northwestern part of China.
( ) 4. The range of temperatures between northern and southern China is quite big in winter.
( ) 5. The Qinling Mountains prevent the cold air masses from spreading to the south.

Task 3 Translation

Directions: *Translate the following passage from Chinese into English.*

总体而言，中国地势西高东低。西部为青藏高原，位于西藏和青海省境内，平均海拔超过4000米，是世界最高地，号称"世界屋脊"。东部海拔450米以下，是中国最繁荣、人口最稠密的地区。北部地势低平，间或为高山阻断；向南是河流冲积而成的平原；再向南是丘陵地带，沟壑纵横。

Task 4 Writing

Directions: *For this part, you are required to write a composition on the topic of* **The National Emblem of the People's Republic of China.**

Section B Listening and Speaking

Text 3 Situational Dialogue: Chinese History

Mark: Guess what I did today!
Li: Called that… what's her name again… and asked her out?
Mark: Come on, give me a break. I've been to the museum. There's an exhibition of ancient Chinese relics.
Li: Sounds great.
Mark: It's fantastic! They look so elaborate and so Chinese! Each item seems to tell a lot about its time.
Li: Taking you back to hundreds or even thousands of years ago.
Mark: Yeah, exactly. But the problem is I've got totally lost about those names of dynasties. Could you straighten it out for me?
Li: Of course. Xia is the first Chinese dynasty. But nothing much is known about it for

lack of archeological evidence.

Mark: Did Xia really exist? Isn't it a legend?

Li: I'm not sure. ① But I believe it once flourished, linking the late Neolithic[1] cultures with the urban civilization of the Shang Dynasty. Shang is the first historically documented dynasty.

Mark: Written on oracle bones[2]?

Li: Right. Then, the Zhou Dynasty began to emerge in the Yellow River valley, overrunning Shang. This period in China was like ancient Greece, a time of incredible development in thought.

Mark: Any great thinkers?

Li: I'm sure you've heard of Confucius and Lao Tzu. And how about *The Art of War*?

Mark: Is it a person's name?

Li: No, it's a book about military laws and tactics of deploying troops. But many sales leaders read it for marketing and negotiation strategies.

Mark: Business is war.

Li: As the power of the Zhou court gradually diminished, the kingdom broke apart into smaller states. Qin was one of them. Its King, Ying Zheng, ended the rivalry among the independent states and established the first centralized, multiethnic state in Chinese history under the Qin Dynasty.

Mark: Wow, he was cool!

Li: He sure was. ② He unified Chinese script, standardized the currency and measures, and built the old Great Wall as well as an extensive network of roads and canals.

Mark: Was he the owner of the terracotta army?

Li: That's right. Those warriors in his tomb were to guard him in the afterlife.

Mark: Impressive.

Li: The Han Dynasty succeeded Qin as the second imperial dynasty. It witnessed further advances in science and culture. Papermaking technique is a great contribution to human civilization. This period also produced China's most famous historian, Sima Qian. His work *Shi Ji* provides a detailed chronicle from the time of a legendary Xia emperor to that of the Han emperor Wu Di.

Mark: Was the Silk Road developed in Han?

Li: Yeah, mainly for trading between China and the Roman Empire. The Han regime existed for over four hundred years. It was followed by the Three Kingdoms Period of Wei, Shu and Wu.

---

1 新石器时代始于距今8000年前的人类原始(母系)氏族的繁荣时期。一般认为新石器时代有三个基本特征：（1）开始制造和使用磨制石器；（2）发明了陶器；（3）出现了原始农业、养畜业和手工业。

2 甲骨文是中国的一种古代文字，被认为是现代汉字的早期形式。甲骨文是商朝（约公元前17世纪—前11世纪）的文化产物，距今约3600多年的历史。

Mark:	Wow, turbulent times for heroes, Cao Cao, Guan Yu, Zhuge Liang …
Li:	*Romance of the Three Kingdoms*? That's not real history.
Mark:	Anyhow, I like it.
Li:	After nearly four centuries of civil wars, the Sui Dynasty managed to reunite China again. The succeeding Tang Dynasty pushed the feudal society to the height of prosperity. China became an expansive, cosmopolitan empire. Its national capital, Chang'an, developed into the world's biggest city at the time.
Mark:	A golden age in Chinese history.
Li:	③ But it began to decline from the middle of the 8th century and another time of political chaos followed till the Song Dynasty ended the divisions and moved to form reunification.
Mark:	I saw a panoramic painting today, rather long, about the city life and landscape along a river…
Li:	*Along the River during the Qingming Festival.*
Mark:	That's it. People from all walks of life jostling for their own businesses … it's amazing!
Li:	After Song, Kublai Khan established the Yuan Dynasty. A book may give you a better view of this period, *The Travels* of *Marco Polo*. In the Yuan Dynasty, there was widespread sentiment against the rule of the Mongolians. Finally they were pushed back to the steppes and replaced by the Ming Dynasty.
Mark:	Was it the last dynasty in Chinese history?
Li:	No, the last one was the Qing Dynasty founded by the Manchus. Anyhow, Ming and Qing dynasties saw unprecedented consolidation and development of China as a unified multiethnic country. It reached its height under the Qianlong Emperor in the eighteenth century, expanding beyond its prior and later boundaries.
Mark:	Wow, a super power!
Li:	But isolated from the outside world and content with the things as they were, it was doomed to decline. The revolution of 1911 overthrew the Qing Dynasty and established the Republic of China.
Mark:	From Xia to Qing, it's really a long history. (779 words)

(Based on: Cao Dawei & Sun Yanjing, 2011, *China's History*, Cengage Learning Asia Pte Ltd.)

Difficult Sentences

① But I believe it once flourished, linking the late Neolithic cultures with the urban civilization of the Shang Dynasty.

不过，我相信它曾兴盛一时，将新石器晚期文化与商朝城市文明连接起来。

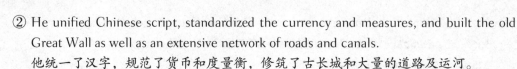

② He unified Chinese script, standardized the currency and measures, and built the old Great Wall as well as an extensive network of roads and canals.

他统一了汉字，规范了货币和度量衡，修筑了古长城和大量的道路及运河。

③ But it began to decline from the middle of the 8th century and another time of political chaos followed till the Song Dynasty ended the divisions and moved to form reunification.

但是它从8世纪中期开始衰落，随后进入了另一段政治混乱时期，直到宋朝结束了分裂继而重新统一了中国。

Text 4 Cities to See in China

Beijing

If you choose to visit only one city in China, it should definitely be Beijing.

The city has been an integral part of China's history over the past eight centuries, and nearly every major building of any age in Beijing has at least some national historical significance. ① The imperial residences and parks, military fortifications, walled hutongs (residential alleys), each is narrating to people its own story in the long course of history. Be in Beijing to visit incredible ancient Forbidden City—the home to China's emperors, marvel at the scale and ingenuity of the Great Wall, and awe at the grandeur of the Temple of Heaven. Besides all these, Beijing is a great source of endless stories and beautiful legends. All awaits your discovery!

Shanghai

Shanghai is the largest city in China. It was one of the first Chinese ports to be opened to

Western trade. Originally a fishing and textile town, Shanghai, due to its favorable port location, flourished to become a multinational center of finance and business by the 1930s. Today it is the largest center of commerce and finance in China.

Shanghai is a fascinating mix of modern and traditional, east and west. With its distinctive architecture and culture, Shanghai enjoys the fame of "Paris of the East". It is popularly seen as the birthplace of everything considered modern in China. The new skyscrapers and old Shikumen[1] lanes together draw the skyline of the city. Western customs and

---

1 石库门是最具上海特色的居民住宅。以石头做门框，以乌漆实心厚木做门扇，这种建筑因此得名"石库门"。

Chinese traditions have intertwined to form Shanghai's culture. Here you will be inspired by the striking contrast between the modern and old Shanghai.

Guangzhou

Known to many in the West as Canton, Guangzhou is famous for foreign trade and business doings, and holds China's largest trade fair, the Canton Fair. Construction of brand new skyscrapers and shopping malls seems a never ending process here. However, there is much history and culture underneath all the glitz and glamour. ② The elegant churches, villas and mansions on the Shamian Island[1], and lovely old residences, temples and gardens hidden among back lanes offer you a time trip to the past.

Of course, it's impossible to talk about Guangzhou without mentioning the food. It's here that you'll try Cantonese cuisine cooked at its very best. The Cantonese will make certain you won't leave their city hungry.

Xi'an

Enjoying equal fame with Athens, Cairo and Rome as one of the four ancient civilization capitals, Xi'an is the cradle of Chinese civilization and the representative of Chinese culture.

World-famous for its Terracotta Warriors — the "Eighth Wonder of the World," the city is filled with amazing historic wonders. It once served as the capital of 13 ancient Chinese dynasties and influenced the world as the eastern start point of the Silk Road. Wandering about the straight and spacious streets encircled by the City Wall, the past of this ancient capital city seems to unfold in front of you. It is a place where you can see the 5,000 years history of China. (503 words)

Difficult Sentences

① The imperial residences and parks, military fortifications, walled hutongs (residential alleys), each is narrating to people its own story in the long course of history.

皇家住宅及园林、军事要塞、胡同，每一处都在向人们讲述它们在漫长的历史进程中所经历的故事。

② The elegant churches, villas and mansions on the Shamian Island, and lovely old residences, temples and gardens hidden among back lanes offer you a time trip to the past.

---

1 沙面岛是广州市独具特色的旅游景点，因中华人民共和国成立前曾长期被英、法等国占为租界，岛上拥有众多欧陆风情的古建筑。

沙面岛上精致的教堂、别墅、府邸，还有藏在僻静小路旁、可爱而古老的住宅、寺庙和花园都能把你带回到过去的时光。

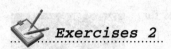

Exercises 2

Task 1 Listening Comprehension

Directions: *Listen to the Situational Dialogue in Text 3, read the four choices marked A, B, C and D, and decide which is the best answer.*

1. The inscriptions on oracle bones verify that _____.
    A. Xia was the first Chinese dynasty
    B. Xia marked the beginning of Chinese urban civilization
    C. Shang was the first historically documented Chinese dynasty
    D. Intellectual life developed significantly in the Shang Dynasty

2. Which is Not true of the Qin Dynasty?
    A. Ying Zheng was the first emperor of a unified China.
    B. A massive national road system was built.
    C. Units of measures were standardized.
    D. It saw a rise of different schools of thought.

3. The Silk Road _____.
    A. was the primary path of commerce for the states along its way
    B. kept nomadic tribes from encroaching on the northern frontiers
    C. led to the decline of the Roman Empire
    D. was ancient trade routes only for silk

4. The Tang Dynasty _____.
    A. witnessed major advances in science and technology
    B. represented a high point in Chinese civilization
    C. was under a powerful cultural influence from neighboring states
    D. acquired a territory larger than any other dynasties

Task 2 Spot Dictation

Directions: *In this section you will hear a passage based on Text 4 three times. When the passage is read for the first time, you should listen carefully for its general idea. When the passage is read for the second time, you are required to fill in the blanks with the exact words you have just heard. Finally, when the passage is read for the third time, you should check what you have written.*

Long serving as the political and cultural center through Chinese history, Beijing is home to many well-preserved imperial residences and parks, military fortifications and (1)_____ alleys. Visitors are impressed by (2)_____ ancient Forbidden City, the scale and ingenuity of the Great Wall, and the grandeur of imperial Temple of Heaven.

Shanghai was one of the first Chinese (3)_____ to be opened to Western trade. It has grown from a fishing and textile town to become the largest center of (4)_____ and finance in China. Having both Western customs and Chinese traditions, new (5)_____ and old Shikumen lanes, the city is a fascinating mix of modern and traditional, east and west.

Guangzhou is famous for foreign trade and business doings. The Canton Fair attracts buyers from all over the world. For lovers of (6)_____, the city offers many other attractions including the elegant churches, villas and mansions on the Shamian Island, and lovely old residences, (7)_____ and gardens hidden among back lanes.

As the cradle of (8)_____, Xi'an is rich in history and culture. It once served as the capital of 13 ancient Chinese dynasties and it was the eastern start point of the Silk Road. The army of (9)_____ is an amazing historic wonder.

Task 3 Short Answer Questions

Directions: *Read Text 3 and Text 4 first, and then answer the following questions briefly.*
1. What is *The Art of War*?
2. Why are there terracotta warriors in the tomb of Ying Zheng?
3. Why was the Qing Dynasty doomed to decline?
4. What makes Beijing one of the most frequently visited cities in China?
5. What is the defining characteristic of Shanghai?

Task 4 Translation

Directions: *Translate the following passage from Chinese into English.*
经过四个世纪的内战，隋朝统一了中国。之后，唐朝将封建社会的繁荣推向顶峰。中国成为一个地域广阔的世界性帝国。这是中华文明史上的黄金时代。8世纪中期，中国国力开始衰退，社会动荡，直到宋朝才得以再度统一。宋之后是元，它的残暴统治激起了民众的仇恨。蒙古统治者因而被赶回大草原，元朝被明朝所替代。

Words and Expressions for Talking about China

Text 1	
Mandarin	*n.* 普通话
character	*n.* 汉字
the Communist Party of China	中国共产党
Tian'anmen Square	天安门
national emblem	国徽
cogwheel	*n.* 齿轮
solidarity	*n.* 团结
ears of grain	麦穗
alliance of industrial and agricultural workers	工农联盟

inauguration	n. 成立典礼；就职典礼
national anthem	国歌
"March of the Volunteers"	《义勇军进行曲》
autonomous region	自治区
municipality	n. 直辖市,自治市
transportation hub	交通枢纽
ethnic group	民族
ethnic minority	少数民族
literacy	n. 有文化，有读写能力
Text 2	
the Pacific Rim	环太平洋
relief	n. 地貌，地面的起伏
mass	n. 气团
the Plateau of Tibet/the Tibetan Plateau	青藏高原
…meters above sea level	海拔……米
the Tarim Basin	塔里木盆地
the Loess Plateau	黄土高原
terrain	n. 地形
flood plain	河漫滩，洪泛平原
topography	n. 地形学，地貌学
tropical monsoon climate	热带季风气候
Text 3	
oracle bone	甲骨
overrun	v. 侵占，打垮
unify Chinese script	统一汉字
standardize the currency and measures	规范货币和度量衡
multiethnic	adj. 多民族的
terracotta army	兵马俑
chaos	n. 混乱
panoramic	adj. 全景的
the Silk Road	丝绸之路
"Along the River during the Qingming Festival"	《清明上河图》
Kublai Khan	忽必烈汗
The Travels of Marco Polo	《马可·波罗游记》

续表

Text 4	
military fortification	军事要塞
residential alley	胡同
Cantonese cuisine	粤菜
Terracotta Warrior	兵马俑

Key to Exercises

Exercises 1

Task 1 Short Answer Questions

1. *March of the Volunteers.*
2. China comprises 23 provinces, five autonomous regions, four municipalities and two special administrative regions.
3. It is located in the eastern part of the Asian continent and on the western Pacific Rim.
4. Because China's relief is roughly high in the west and low in the east.
5. The Plateau of Tibet.

Task 2 Reading Comprehension

Part A
1. deposits   2. lofty   3. unveiled   4. inauguration   5. plain

Part B
1. E   2. D   3. E   4. C   5. C

Task 3 Translation

Broadly speaking, the relief of China is high in the west and low in the east. The west area is represented by the Plateau of Tibet, located in Tibet and Qinghai, with an average elevation of over 4000 meters. It is the highest part in the world and is termed as "the roof of the world". The east area, with an elevation below 450 meters, is the most prosperous and populous in China. In the north lies a low and flat land, occasionally interrupted by the mountains. Southward, one could see plains created by the rivers. In the far south, there are hills crossed by the river valleys.

Task 4 Writing

Sample Writing

The National Emblem of the People's Republic of China

The national emblem of the People's Republic of China shows Tian'anmen under the light of five stars. Tian'anmen is the symbol of modern China because the May Fourth Movement of 1919, which marked the beginning of the new-democratic revolution in China, was launched there. It is also the place where Mao Zedong declared the foundation of P.R.C. in 1949. The five stars can be found on the national flag. The largest star represents the Communist Party of China, while the four smaller stars represent the four social classes as defined in Maoism. The outer circle has a border that contains sheaves of wheat and the inner sheaves of rice, which represents agricultural workers. At the center of the bottom portion of the border is a cogwheel that represents the industrial workers.

These elements together were designed to symbolize the birth of New China and the people's democratic dictatorship led by the working class and based on the alliance of the industrial and agricultural workers.

The emblem was officially made the national emblem on September 20, 1950, by the Central People's Government. (190 words)

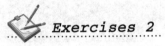

Exercises 2

Task 1 Listening Comprehension
1. C   2. D   3. A   4. B

Task 2 Spot Dictation
1. residential
2. incredible
3. ports
4. commerce
5. skyscrapers
6. architecture
7. temples
8. Chinese civilization
9. Terracotta Warriors

Task 3 Short Answer Questions
1. It's a book about military laws and tactics of deploying troops.
2. The warriors were believed able to guard the king in his afterlife.
3. Because it was isolated from the outside world and content with the things as they were.
4. It has been an integral part of China's history over the past eight centuries.
5. A mix of modern and traditional.

Task 4 Translation
After four centuries of civil wars, the Sui Dynasty reunited China. The succeeding Tang Dynasty pushed the feudal society to the peak of its prosperity. China became an expansive, cosmopolitan empire. That was the golden age in Chinese civilization. In the middle of the 8th century, it began to decline and slipped into chaos. The state was not reunited until the establishment of the Song Dynasty. After Song, the Yuan Dynasty came into being, and its ruthless rule induced hatred from the public. Consequently, the Mongolians were pushed back to the steppes and the Yuan Dynasty was replaced by the Ming Dynasty.

Unit 2 Chinese People

> **导 读**
>
> 中华民族历史悠久，各族人民共同创建了伟大的中华文明。本单元旨在通过对主要民族的语言、文化、建筑等方面进行介绍，使学生能够运用所学中国文化知识及相关的英语表达进行跨文化交流，让世界了解中华民族。

Before You Start

While you are preparing for this unit, think about the following questions:
1. How many ethnic groups do you know there are in China? Can you list their names?
2. Apart from standard Chinese—Mandarin or Putonghua, many people in China can speak a local dialect. How many major dialects are spoken in China? Please name at least 3 dialects.

Section A Reading and Writing

Text 1 Han People

China, with more than 1.4 billion people, is the most populous country in the world. As a large united multi-ethnic state, it is composed of 56 ethnic groups. Among them, Han people accounted for 91.11% of the overall Chinese population and the other 55 minorities made up the remaining 8.89% according to the Seventh National Population Census in 2020.

The name Han comes from the Han Dynasty, whose first emperor was originally known as the king of the region of Hanzhong, which is where the word is derived.

Among some southern Han people, a different term "tangren" exists within various Chinese dialects like Cantonese, Hakka and Minnan. Tangren, literally "Tang people," comes from a later Chinese dynasty, the Tang Dynasty, another zenith of Chinese civilization. It is used in everyday conversation and also an element in the Cantonese dialect for Chinatown (tangrenjie), literally "Tang people's street (s)."

For thousands of years, Han people, together with other ethnic minorities, have made outstanding achievements in the spheres of politics, philosophy, art, literature and natural science.

Language

Han people speak various forms of hanyu, literally "Han language," and write Chinese hanzi, literally "Chinese characters." Although the residents of different regions would not necessarily understand each other's speech because of their dialects, they generally share a common written language. As the oldest known recorded language written on old bones and turtle shells, Chinese language is not alphabetic, and a large number of its characters are ideographic symbols, representing the oldest writing system in the world. The monosyllabic structure, the open vocabulary nature, the flexible wording structure with tones, and the flexibilities in word ordering are good examples of the structural features of Chinese language.

Religion and Belief

Confucianism, not a religion but an ideology, has been influencing and shaping the whole Chinese society and people, especially Han people, for thousands of years. Taoism, the only religion native to China, and Buddhism, originally introduced from India, are the main religions of the Han people. Some people also belong to various Christian denominations due to the influence of Western culture.

Names

The names of Han people are typically two or three syllables in length, with the surname preceding the given name. ① Surnames are typically one character in length, though a few uncommon surnames are two or more syllables long, while given names are one or two syllables long. Now there are about 3,000 surnames in China, of which about 100 surnames are most common. Besides the common culture and writings, common origin rooted in the surnames is another major factor that contributes to the identity of Han people.

Food and Food Culture

The staple food of Han is rice and wheat. ② Rice is versatile and can be served in a variety of ways including porridge, rice cake, glutinous rice dumpling and rice noodles. Wheat is used in the production of steamed bread, noodles, steamed stuffed buns, dumplings and wonton. Han people living in different regions of China have developed unique styles of cooking. The eight cuisines are the representative. Tea and alcohol are Chinese traditional drinks. Han Chinese like to entertain their honored guests with them.

Housing

House styles and materials of Han people vary in different regions of China. Those built in north China are mostly made of bricks in the courtyard style. The courtyard (siheyuan) in Beijing is a representative.

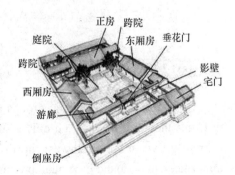

However, in southern China, Han people build their houses mainly of timber. The unique style of their buildings can be admired in the earthen buildings in Fujian and the pavilions in Suzhou. All the houses of Han are suggested to be positioned in the north facing south to catch the maximum sunlight.

Along with the fast urbanization, an increasing number of Han people move to cities and live in modern buildings.

Clothing

Today, Han people usually wear Western-style or modern clothing. Few wear traditional Han Chinese clothing on a regular basis. It is, however, preserved in religious and ceremonial costumes.

In recent years, hanfu fashion has become increasingly popular with young people as a symbol of Chinese traditional culture and a way to reconnect themselves with traditions.

Now, the most popular traditional Chinese clothing worn by many women on important occasions such as wedding banquets and New Year is called qipao. However, this attire comes not from the Han people but from a modified fashion style of the Manchus, an ethnic group that ruled China between 1644 and 1912.

Festivals

Festivals of Han people are rich and colorful. The most important ones are the Spring Festival (the 1st day of the 1st lunar month), the Lantern Festival (the 15th day of the 1st lunar month), the Dragon Boat Festival (the 5th day of the 5th lunar month) and the Mid-autumn Festival (the 15th day of 8th lunar month) according to Chinese lunar calendar. (802 words)

 Difficult Sentences

① Surnames are typically one character in length, though a few uncommon surnames are two or more syllables long, while given names are one or two syllables long.
虽然一些特殊的姓氏包含两个或更多汉字，但是汉姓一般只有一个字，名字由一个或两个字组成。

② Rice is versatile and can be served in a variety of ways including porridge, rice cake, glutinous rice dumpling and rice noodles.
稻米的功能很多，可以做成各种各样的食物，比如粥、年糕、糯米团子和米粉。

Text 2 A Glimpse of Chinese 55 Ethnic Minorities

① The 55 minority ethnic groups are distributed extensively throughout different regions of China though they make up only a small proportion of the overall Chinese population. They primarily live in the southwest, northwest and northeast of China. The greatest number of minorities can be found in Yunnan province (25 ethnic groups).

The Chinese government has introduced a series of policies to secure the equality, unity and harmony of its 56 ethnic groups, and regional autonomy for ethnic minorities is the most fundamental of them. Five autonomous regions, namely Inner Mongolia, Xinjiang Uygur, Guangxi Zhuang, Ningxia Hui and Tibet, as well as numerous autonomous prefectures, counties, nationality townships and towns, have been set up. They are entitled autonomy to govern and deal with their own affairs. Together with Han people, the ethnic minorities have been making great efforts to build a prosperous China.

Generally, each ethnic minority has its unique characteristics such as languages, costumes and customs different from other minority groups as well as Han people, but there are also some that are very similar to the Han majority group, for example, Manchu and Hui. Some minorities are introduced here.

Hui People

Hui is China's most widely distributed ethnic minority. Small-scale concentration and wide distribution are the characteristics of their inhabitation. A large number of them settle in Ningxia Hui autonomous region. Immigrants from Central Asia increased their numbers during the Yuan Dynasty (1271—1368). Islamism has played a vital role in their development, influencing them in all walks of life.

Chinese is the shared language of Hui people. Some Arabic and Persian words are also used in daily interactions and religious activities. Mosques are the symbol of architecture in large Hui communities. Eid al-Fitr (Festival of Breaking Fast) and Eid al-Adha (Festival of Sacrifice) are their main festivals.

Mongolian People

The Mongolian hordes of Genghis Khan and his successors swept as far as Vienna in the 14th century. Most Mongolians are now found in Inner Mongolia autonomous region. Mandarin Chinese is used, while they have their own spoken and written language, which belongs to the Mongolian branch of the Altaic language system. Livestock, coal, iron, salt, steel, and grain are economically important, yet many Mongols remain semi-nomadic. They follow their flocks in summer, covering great distances and living in tents called yurts. ② Their yearly Nadam Fair features stock sales, contests of horsemanship, wrestling, and archery.

Tibetan People

As an old ethnic group of China, Tibetan people mainly live in Tibet autonomous region, and its neighboring provinces: Qinghai, Gansu, Sichuan and Yunnan. They have their own spoken and written language which belongs to Cambodian branch, Sino-Tibetan language system.

Mainly living on farming and stock raising, most Tibetan people are devout

Buddhists, and observe Tibetan Buddhism. Lamaseries spread all over Tibetan areas, and exhibit the rich culture and superb construction skill of Tibetans. ③ The Potala Palace on Mt. Hongshan (Marpo Ri) in Lhasa, the capital city of Tibet, is the palace complex with the highest altitude in the world.

Zanba, mutton and beef are their staple food. In some areas, rice and noodles are also a regular part of their diet. Tea with butter or milk, yoghourt and cheese are the favorites of all Tibetans.

Uygur People

Uygur people mainly settle in Xinjiang Uygur autonomous region of China. Their history can be traced back as far as Huihe people of the Tang Dynasty. The Silk Road threading through Xinjiang's deserts and mountains carried China's trade westward and also brought Islam to the Uygur. Most Uygur people speak the Uygur language and for centuries use Arabic script.

The Uygur mainly live on agriculture by raising stock and growing fruit, wheat, cotton, and rice. As the largest producer of grapes in China, they cultivate large quantities of grapes in the Turpan Basin. Many people also work in state-run crafts and textile factories, or carpets mills. Rice, wheat and some mixed grain are their staple food and they usually eat beef, mutton, and chicken.

Zhuang People

Zhuang people, whose origin goes back well before the time of Christ, is the most populous of China's minorities. Over 90 percent of its people live in Guangxi Zhuang autonomous region. They speak the Zhuang language, but many speak Chinese. They primarily grow rice and corn,

and poached and pickled vegetables are their favorite.

④ Zhuang brocade is one of the four famous Chinese brocades, and renowned for its color, luster, durability and the wide range of use. Zhuang's frescoes and bronze drums are also of splendid fame.

Their unique festivals include: the Devil Festival (July 14), the Ox Soul Festival (April 8), and the Singing Festival (March 3) on Chinese lunar calendar. (776 words)

Difficult Sentences

① The 55 minority ethnic groups are distributed extensively throughout different regions of China though they make up only a small proportion of the overall Chinese population.
尽管55个少数民族只占了中国总人口的一小部分，他们却广泛分布于中国的各个地区。

② Their yearly Nadam Fair features stock sales, contests of horsemanship, wrestling, and archery.
每年那达慕大会的主要内容是牲畜买卖，以及比赛骑马、摔跤和射箭。（蒙古语中那达慕为娱乐或游戏的意思）

③ The Potala Palace on Mt. Hongshan (Marpo Ri) in Lhasa, the capital city of Tibet, is the palace complex with the highest altitude in the world.
布达拉宫坐落在西藏首府拉萨的红山（藏语叫玛布日山）上，是世界上海拔最高的宫殿群。

④ Zhuang brocade is one of the four famous Chinese brocades, and renowned for its color, luster, durability and the wide range of use.
壮锦是中国四大织锦之一，以其色泽度、耐用性和用途广而知名。

Exercises 1

Task 1 Short Answer Questions

Directions: *Read Text 1 and Text 2 and then answer the following questions briefly.*

1. Why does Han people, the biggest ethnic group in China, address itself as "Han" people?
2. What's the major characteristic of Han people's language, hanyu?
3. What is the biggest festival in China?
4. What's the policy of China for its ethnic minorities?
5. Who are the ancestors of Uygur people and what's their religion?

Task 2 Reading Comprehension
Part A

Directions: *In this section, there are 5 incomplete sentences. You are required to select one word for each blank from a list of choices given in the word bank below. You may not use any of the words in the bank more than once.*

| philosophy | delighted | residents | rewarded | contented |
| awarded | foreign | residences | religion | overseas |

1. The Chinese usually identify a person by his ethnic origin instead of nationality. As long as he is of Chinese descent (血统), he is considered Chinese, and if he lives outside of China, he is a(an) _____ Chinese.

2. In 2012, Mo Yan was _____ the Nobel Prize in Literature for his work as a writer "who with hallucinatory (魔幻的) realism merges folk tales, history and the contemporary."

3. Chinese people are peaceful, reserved, humble, hardworking and easily _____. They respect elders, love children and are patient with their fellows.

4. The reason why Chinese people do not feel the need of a religion is that they have belief in Confucianism, a system of _____ and ethics, a synthesis (综合) of human society and civilization which can take the place of religion.

5. Courtyard houses of north China, with Beijing's siheyuan (courtyard with houses on all sides) most typical, are the outstanding representatives of traditional _____ of China's Han people.

Part B

Directions: *In this section, you are going to read a passage with five statements attached to it. Each statement contains information given in one of the paragraphs. Identify the paragraph from which the information is derived. Each paragraph is marked with a letter.*

A) The names of Chinese people have their own tradition and characteristics. Unlike the Westerners', the family name in China is put at the beginning of a whole name, followed by the given name. Generally, a female does not use her husband's family name. The given name usually contains one or two Chinese characters, but in order to avoid confusion, newly-born babies are now entitled to given names of three characters.

B) Chinese names are meant to convey special meanings, with the given names often expressing the best wishes for the newborn babies. Some imply the birthplaces, birth time or natural phenomena, like Jing (Beijing), Chen (morning), and Xue (snow), some embody the hopes of virtues, like Zhong (faithfulness) and Xin (reliability) while others express the wishes of life, such as Jian (health) and Fu (happiness).

C) Among all the family names, 100 common ones cover almost 87% of the total population. Of these, 19 are more popular than the others, including Li, Wang, Zhang, Liu, Chen, Yang, Zhao, Huang, Zhou, Wu, Xu, Sun, Hu, Zhu, Gao, Lin, He, Guo and Ma, and they represent about half of the whole Chinese people. Some Chinese have compound surnames, consisting of two characters, such as Ouyang, Shangguan, Sima and Nangong. Now there are altogether 81 compound surnames existing in the country.

D) All Chinese people have equal rights to use their own names, which are legally protected. Generally speaking, a child is always entitled to the surname of his father. However, children nowadays in China do not have to do so; they can also adopt surnames of their mothers. Nicknames are often called in their childhood or by their confidants (密友).

E) It is considered polite and respectful to address a Chinese by his/her surname, followed by honorific titles like xiansheng (Sir), nvshi (Madam) or the job position. Given names are often called between good friends.

( ) 1. It is polite to address a man as xiansheng.
( ) 2. Nowadays, children can adopt their mothers' family names.
( ) 3. In Chinese names, family names are put before given names.
( ) 4. Chinese names generally have special meanings.
( ) 5. Compound first/family names with two characters are also found in China.

Task 3 Translation

Directions: *Translate the following passage from Chinese into English.*

汉语又称中文、普通话，属汉藏语系，是世界上作为母语使用人数最多的语言，约有15亿使用者。它是联合国六种工作语言之一。在中国，尽管不同地区的人们会说方言，但是全国使用统一的书面文字汉语。作为世界上最古老的文字之一，汉语不是字母文字，而是由很多表意汉字组成的文字。

Task 4 Writing

Directions: *According to UNESCO, more than half of the 6000 languages in the world are facing extinction. In China, most ethnic minorities have their own languages but some of them are facing extinction, for example, the Mosuo language and the Ewenki language. Write an essay on* **Endangered Languages of Chinese Ethnic Minorities**.

Section B Listening and Speaking

Text 3 Situational Dialogue: Modern Chinese Youth

(A: Host of a radio program   B: Guest—Li Jun, a sociologist)

A: Hello, Mr. Li, welcome to our program "People in China." The topic today is about Chinese youth. What do you think of Chinese youth as a group?

B: Thank you! As an emerging mainstream, Chinese young people are demonstrating great vitality, innovation and responsibility. Nowadays you can find many excellent young people in various fields, for example, business, science, government, sports, arts...

A: That's true! Though a small group of people are not that independent of their parents, most young people are independent and confident. Is that because they are more educated?

B: Definitely yes. When young people receive a higher education, they know more about the world and themselves, cultivate more good virtues and moralities, and become more tolerable of diversities. They also acquire more professional knowledge and silks for better jobs. So education is extremely important to all people.

A: Other factors boosting the youth's morale?

B: A major one is the fast development of Chinese economy. It is the fundamental reason why all of us are more confident than before.

A: Now let's look at some representatives of the young people. China ranked first, second and second in the total number of gold medals in Beijing 2008 Olympic games, London 2012 Olympic Games, and Tokyo 2020 Olympic Games, respectively. China ranked third in total medals in Beijing 2022 Olympic Winter Games and made an important leap in winter sports. What do you think of modern young sports players?

B: Young sports players, especially those gold medal winners from the Olympic Games, are role models for young people. They not only exhibit great athletic expertise and persistence on sports playgrounds, but also show good personal moralities on and off the courts.

A: For example?

B: For example, Yao Ming. His brilliant basketball skills bring him great popularity, but his modesty wins him more fans. Of course, we can't forget the well-known diving "Dream Team" and many new stars like Zhu Ting, Pan Zhendong, Chen Meng, Gu Ailing, Zhang Mengxue, Ding Junhui…

A: We know the achievements in science may be the strongest force driving the social advancement. Can you name a few young scientists in China?

B: Yeah. There are a lot of promising young scientists. For example, Cao Yuan, a new star studying the super-conductivity of graphene (石墨烯), and Lu Cewu, an expert in AI's visual detection.

A: Then how about art circles?

B: The pianist Langlang. He shows the world that the Chinese can also be excellent piano players.

A: Then in business and technology industry?

B: In recent years, there have been emerging more and more talented and successful young entrepreneurs. A large number of young people work hard developing different technologies, for example, 5G, AI, electromagnetic levitation, aerospace, supercomputing, biopharmaceuticals (生物制药) and so on.

A: Now let's come to common folks. How do you like average young people?

B: Average Chinese youth are as great as their well-known inspiring peer representatives. For example, in the forest fire that broke out in Liangshan prefecture, Sichuan province on March 30, 2019, 27 young forest firefighters died for putting out the fire. In the critical moments when COVID-19 pandemic broke out and raged on in 2020, many young doctors, nurses and other medical workers volunteered to work in the front line at risk of their lives. Thousands of young policemen and community staff also worked day and night. Many young medical scientists tried to develop COVID-19 vaccines without a break. All of them show great responsibility and dedication.

A: Now more and more young people belong to the only-child generation spoiled by their parents. It is especially precious of them to be so selfless and brave. They are the real heroes and role models among us, the future backbone of China.

B: Yes!

A: Chinese women are often described as "half the sky" of the society. Their contribution to the society cannot be ignored. So what do you think of modern Chinese young women?

B: Oh, they are very diligent and brilliant. They study and work harder than their male peers to earn them a place in the highly competitive society. As a result, their efforts pay off. There are so many excellent examples, Liu Yang, the first Chinese female astronaut having traveled in the space, Zhou Chengyu, the youngest female commander of Chang'e-5 Launching Project, Tan Fanglin, the youngest female scientist, Zhang Jingjing, the most beautiful nurse who died in assisting Wuhan to combat the epidemic …

A: An endless list! We believe that Chinese young people are constructing and will build a more prosperous China. That's the end of today's program. Thank you for having come to us, Mr. Li!

B: My pleasure. Thank you! (787 words)

Related Expressions

1. The person's age, sex, appearance, personality, education, family background, jobs and achievements…are factors that should be included in your dialogue. 对话应该包括该人的年龄、性别、外貌、性格、教育、家庭背景、工作和成就等内容。

2. Personality: charming, easy-going, out-going, optimistic/pessimistic (乐观的/悲观的), independent, helpful, reserved (矜持含蓄的), introverted/extroverted (内向/外向的), tolerant (容忍的)

3. Education and family background: literate (有文化的/受过教育的), illiterate (没有文化的/文盲的), well-educated, poorly-educated, from a rich/poor/average family, receive a good family education, a big/small/harmonious family

4. Occupation: artist, painter, director (导演), TV producer (电视制作人), disc jockey (D.J.) (电台的音乐节目主持人), master of ceremonies (M.C.) (节目主持人，司仪), musician, fashion designer (时装设计师), editor (编辑), chief editor (主编), photographer (摄影师), journalist/reporter (记者), photo journalist (摄影记者), astronaut (宇航员), chemist (药剂师), technician (技师), barber (理发师), tour guide, coach (教练), sanitation engineer ([美委婉语]垃圾清洁工), life guard (救生员), firefighter (消防人员), dentist (牙医), physician (内科医师), surgeon (外科医生), psychiatrist (精神病医师), psychologist (心理学家), veterinarian/vet (兽医), customs officer (海关官员), flight attendant (飞机上的服务员), pilot (飞行员), architect (建筑师), civil engineer (土木工程师), construction worker (建筑工人), maintenance engineer (维修工程师), consultant (顾问), secretary, supervisor (主管), receptionist (接待员)

Text 4 Mosuo People—A Matriarchal Society

① The Mosuo are descendants of ancient Qiang people and they are classified as a subgroup of the Naxi people because the languages of the two groups are similar. The group has a population of about 50,000 people. The Mosuo are distributed in Yunnan and Sichuan provinces, but most of them live in Yongning, a town in Lijiang of Yunnan Province, and around Lugu Lake, their "mother lake."

The Mosuo speak a dialect of the Naxi language, a member of the Tibetan-Burman family. They use Han script for daily communication and Tibetan script for religious purposes.

Mosuo people are primarily engaged in agriculture and they are largely self-sufficient in diet. They raise livestock and grow crops. They are renowned for their preserved pork, which may be kept for 10 years or more. They also produce a local alcoholic beverage made from grain, called sulima, which is similar to strong wine. Sulima is drunk regularly and usually offered to guests at ceremonies and festivals.

The Mosuo culture is frequently described as matriarchal. They have aspects of a matriarchal culture: women are often the head of the house, inheritance is through the female line, and women make business decisions. ② It has been considered as the living fossil as a basis for studying social patterns and matriarchal marriage customs in today's world.

A typical Mosuo family includes a grandmother, mothers, uncles, sisters, younger brothers, older brothers and sisters' children. The matriarch (ami in Chinese) is the head of the house. She has absolute power and decides the fate of all those living under her roof. She manages the money and jobs of each family member. When she wishes to pass her duties on to the next generation, she will give this female successor the keys to the household storage, and it signifies the passing on of property rights and responsibility.

Mosuo women do almost everything. They raise crops and stock, take care of their children, and earn money. Men are responsible for some heavy tasks such as plowing, clearing land, herding horses and hauling fish nets and occasionally help out at stores and guest houses owned by the women. Mostly they sit around, play pool and watch the children.

Mosuo men and women are not bound by marriage, each living at their mothers' home. The man-woman relationship in Mosuo culture is called "walking marriage" or "visiting relation" based on mutual affection. When a Mosuo woman or man expresses interest in a potential partner, it is the woman who may give the man permission to visit her. These visits are usually kept secret: the man visits the woman's house after dark, spends the night, and returns to his own home in the morning. Mosuo women and men can engage in such relations with different partners they love, but not at the same time. Walking marriages are free from social pressures and allow more independence.

③ While a pairing may be long-term, the man seldom lives with the woman's family, or vice versa. Mosuo men and women continue to live with and be responsible for their respective families. The couple do not share property. The father usually has little responsibility for his offspring. It is the job of men to care more for their nieces and nephews than for their own children. A father may indicate an interest in the upbringing of his children by bringing gifts to the mother's family. This gives him status within the mother's family, while not actually

becoming part of the family. Whether or not the father is involved, children are raised in the mother's home and assume her family name. (608 words)

Difficult Sentences

① The Mosuo are descendants of ancient Qiang people and they are classified as a subgroup of the Naxi people because the languages of the two groups are similar.
摩梭人是古羌人的后代；因为和纳西族使用的语言相似，它又被划分为纳西族的一支。

② It has been considered as the living fossil as a basis for studying social patterns and matriarchal marriage customs in today's world.
摩梭人被看作活化石，是研究当今社会结构和母系婚俗的基础。

③ While a pairing may be long-term, the man seldom lives with the woman's family, or vice versa.
虽然男女交往可能持续较长时间，但男方很少和女方的家人住在一起，女方也不会入住男方家。

Exercises 2

Task 1 Listening Comprehension

Directions: Listen to the Situational Dialogue in Text 3, read the four choices marked A, B, C and D, and decide which is the best answer.

1. What does the program guest Mr. Li do?
   A. He is a psychologist.   B. He is a sociologist.
   C. He is a news reporter.   D. He is one of the great youth in China.
2. What are the main characteristics of modern Chinese youth as a group?
   A. They show great vitality.   B. They show great innovation.
   C. They show great responsibility.   D. All of the above.
3. What mostly contribute to modern Chinese youth's independence and confidence?
   A. Improvement of their education and the fast development of Chinese economy.
   B. Improvement of their life quality and better care from their parents.
   C. Cultivation of good virtues and moralities.
   D. Acquirement of more skills.
4. Some sports players are role models for the youth because _____.
   A. they perform professionally on courts
   B. they persist in their sports
   C. they behave morally off courts
   D. All of the above

5. Why are Chinese women described as "half the sky" of the society?
   A. Because they take up half of the whole population in China.
   B. Because they are the other gender of the society.
   C. Because they work very hard to earn their own places and make great contribution to the social development.
   D. Because they do much better than Chinese men.

Task 2 Spot Dictation

Directions: *You will hear the passage taken from Text 4 three times. When the passage is read for the first time, you should listen carefully for its general idea. When the passage is read for the second time, you are required to fill in the blanks with the exact words you have just heard. Finally, when the passage is read for the third time, you should check what you have written.*

The Mosuo are descendants of ancient Qiang people and they are (1)_____ a subgroup of the Naxi people because the languages of the two groups are similar. The group has a (2)_____ of about 50,000 people. The Mosuo are distributed in Yunnan and Sichuan provinces, close to the border with Tibet, but most of them live in Yongning, a town in Lijiang of Yunnan (3)_____, and around the Lugu Lake, their "mother lake."

The Mosuo speak a dialect of the Naxi language, a member of the Tibetan-Burman family (藏缅语族). They use Han script for daily communication and Tibetan script for (4)_____ purposes.

Mosuo people are primarily (5)_____ agriculture and they are largely self-sufficient in diet. They raise livestock and grow crops. They are renowned for their (6)_____ pork, which may be kept for 10 years or more. They also produce a local alcoholic beverage made from grain, called sulima, which is similar to strong wine. Sulima is drunk regularly and usually offered to guests at ceremonies and (7)_____.

The Mosuo culture is frequently described as matriarchal. They have (8)_____ a matriarchal culture: women are often the head of the house, inheritance is through the (9)_____ line, and women make business decisions. It has been considered as the living fossil as a basis for studying social patterns and matriarchal marriage (10)_____ in today's world.

Task 3 Short Answer Questions

Directions: *Read Text 4 and briefly answer the following questions.*
1. Who are the ancestors of Mosuo people?
2. Which lake is Mosuo people's "mother lake"?
3. How do most Mosuo people make a living?
4. What are the features of a matriarchal family?
5. What is Mosuo people's "walking marriage" like?

Task 4 Translation

Directions: *Translate the following passage from Chinese into English.*
摩梭人是古羌人的后裔，生活在云南省西北与四川省交界处风光秀丽的泸沽湖畔，人口约五万，有自己的语言，但没有文字。住在金沙江东部的摩梭人的语言、服饰、婚姻习俗与金沙江西部的纳西族有差异。摩梭人是中国唯一仍存在的母系氏族社会，实行独特的"男不娶，女不嫁"的"走婚"制度。

Words and Expressions for Chinese People

Text 1	
multi-ethnic state	多民族国家
the Seventh National Population Census	第7次全国人口普查
be derived from	源自
zenith	*n.* 鼎盛时期
ethnic group	民族
ethnic minority	少数民族
Chinese character	汉字
ideographic	*adj.* 表意的
monosyllabic	*adj.* 单音节的
inscriptions on bones or turtle shells	*n.* 甲骨文
denomination	*n.* （基督教）教派，宗派
Taoism/Daoism	*n.* 道教
Confucianism	*n.* 儒家思想
Buddhism	*n.* 佛教
the Book of Family Names	百家姓
staple food	主食
courtyard house/ siheyuan	四合院
earthen building	土楼
national costume	民族服装
attire	*n.* 服饰
the Spring Festival Fair	庙会
the Soring Festival/the Chinese New Year	春节
Text 2	
extensively distribute	广泛分布
Ningxia Hui autonomous region	宁夏回族自治区
Islam	*n.* 伊斯兰教
all walks of life	各行各业
mosque	清真寺
Arabic	*adj.* 阿拉伯语的，阿拉伯的
Persian	*adj.* 波斯语的，波斯的

Eid al-Fitr	开斋节
Eid al-Adha	古尔邦节
horde	n. 游牧民族
Genghis Khan	成吉思汗
Inner Mongolia autonomous region	内蒙古自治区
livestock	n. 牲畜
archery	n. 射箭，箭术
Tibetan Buddhism	藏传佛教
lamasery	n. 喇嘛寺
the Potala Palace	布达拉宫
devout Buddhist	虔诚的佛教徒
the Uygur/Uygur people	n. 维吾尔族人
the Turpan Basin	吐鲁番盆地
textile factory	纺织厂
state-run enterprise	国有企业
Text 3	
good virtues and moralities	美德
role model	榜样
on/off sports playground	运动场上/下
graphene	石墨烯
single-child generation	独生子女一代
half the sky	半边天
male peer	男同胞
highly competitive society	竞争激烈的社会
world chess champion	国际象棋世界冠军
earn sb. a place	为……赢得一席之地
Text 4	
matriarchal society	母系氏族社会
descendent	n. 后代
Tibetan nomad	西藏游牧民族
subgroup/branch	n. 分支
be engaged in agriculture	从事农业劳动
self-sufficient in diet	饮食自给自足
alcoholic beverage	酒精饮料

续表

rice wine	米酒
ceremony	*n.* 仪式和节日
marriage custom	婚俗
living fossil	活化石
successor	*n.* 继承人
walking/visiting marriage	走婚

Key to Exercises

Task 1 Short Answer Questions
1. Because the name Han comes from Han Dynasty and its first emperor was originally known as king of the region of Hanzhong. So Hanzhong, Han Dynasty and Han people.
2. Hanyu or Han language is not alphabetic but ideographic, and it has monosyllabic structure, open vocabulary, and flexible wording structure with tones and wording ordering.
3. The Spring Festival. It is celebrated by all Han people and some other ethnic minorities.
4. To secure equality, unity, and harmony of its 56 ethnic groups, China' fundamental policy for the other 55 ethnic minorities is regional autonomy. They are entitled autonomy to govern and handle their own affairs.
5. Their ancestors are nomadic Huihe people in Tang Dynasty, and they believe in Islam.

Task 2 Reading Comprehension
Part A
1. overseas   2. awarded   3. contented   4. philosophy   5. residences

Part B
1. E   2. D   3. A   4. B   5. C

Task 3 Translation
Hanyu, also known as Chinese and mandarin (putonghua), is a part of Sino-Tibetan language family. It is the language with the largest number of native speakers in the world, with about 1.5 billion users. It is one of the six working languages of the United Nations. Although people in different regions of China speak dialects, unified written Chinese is used across the country. As one of the oldest languages in the world, Chinese is not alphabetic, but composed of many ideographic Chinese characters.

Task 4 Writing
Sample Writing

Endangered Languages of Chinese Ethnic Minorities
An endangered language is a language at the risk of falling out of use as its speakers die out or shift to speaking another language. Some Chinese ethnic minorities are facing the fact of losing their native languages.

Many factors contribute to this phenomenon. In a general sense, globalization is quickening its step cutting down on varieties of different nations, cultures and languages and shaping the world in an assimilated mode. For example, more young people leave their hometowns for cities for jobs, forgetting their native languages and meanwhile reducing the population of their ethnic groups.

A language is the carrier of the knowledge, culture and experience accumulated by a nation or a group throughout history. Losing the language is like losing a group's identity and its rich culture. It is an irretrievable loss to the nation and the whole world.

Therefore, it is of great significance to protect and preserve such endangered languages. Both Chinese central government and the local governments should encourage minority peoples to speak and use their own languages. Linguists should help create written languages for certain ethnic groups and the people of these ethnic groups should have an awareness to protect their languages and try to use and develop them in daily life. (214 words)

Exercises 2

Task 1 Listening Comprehension
1. B   2. D   3. A   4. D   5. C

Task 2 Spot Dictation
1. classified as   2. population   3. province   4. religious   5. engaged in
6. preserved   7. festivals   8. aspects of   9. female   10. customs

Task 3 Short Answer Questions
1. Ancient Qiang People.
2. The Lugu Lake.
3. They mainly make a living on agriculture.
4. In a matriarchal family, women are often the head of the house, inheritance is through the female line and women make business decisions.
5. A walking marriage, also called visiting marriage, is based on mutual interest and love of men and women and it gives them more independence and less pressure. They don't get married but men visit women during nights and leave in the morning.

Task 4 Translation
As descendants of ancient Qiang people, the Mosuo dwell around the Lugu Lake, which is located on the bordering of Yunan province's northwest and Sichuan province. With about 50,000 people, the Musuo has its language, only verbal but not written. The Mosuo who reside along the eastern side of the Jinsha River demonstrate a sharp contrast in language, costume and marriage conventions from the Naxi tribes living on the western side of the River. The Mosuo live in the only matriarchal society in China that persists to this day, and it maintains a unique "visiting marriage" system.

Unit 3

Chinese Language and Literature

> **导　读**
>
> 本单元旨在通过对当代中国文学作品的简要介绍，深化学生对中国文学精髓的理解，掌握相应的英文表达，能在对外交流过程中更好地宣扬本民族的文学与文化。

Before You Start

While you are preparing for this unit, think about the following questions:

1. Have you ever read any novels written by Jin Yong, or watched any TV series or movies adapted from his works? Which character in his works impresses you most?
2. What is the first short story written by Lu Xun in the vernacular language (白话文)? What is it about?

Section A　Reading and Writing

Text 1 Jin Yong, a Literary Swordsman

Jin Yong is one of the most famous and popular novelists in China nowadays. His works of "Wuxia" (martial arts and chivalry) enjoys a widespread popularity in Chinese-speaking areas. He is a best-selling Chinese author; over 100 million copies of his works have been sold worldwide, not including unknown number of bootleg copies.

"Jin Yong" is the pen name of Cha Leung Yung, also known as Louis Cha for the name appearing on the covers of the English version of some of his books. He was born on February 6, 1924 in Haining, Zhengjiang province, in Southeastern China. In 1950, Cha Leung Yung, who worked as an editor for the *Ta*

Kung Pao in Hong Kong, began his writing of Wuxia novels. He adopted the pen name of "Jin Yong". From that time to 1972, the year when he announced the ending of his novel writing, he completed a total of 14 novels of various lengths. Each of these works became popular after their publication and nearly all of them have been adapted into TV series, movies, comic books as well as computer games. Now 40 years after his announcement of ceasing writing, his works are still on the best-seller list of book stores in China.

Interestingly, the first characters of the titles of his 14 works can be joined together to form a couplet with 7 characters in each line. By remembering the couplet, fans of Jin Yong can easily recall the titles of all his works: "飞雪连天射白鹿，笑书神侠倚碧鸳."

① Most of his works, though fictional, are set in the real historical periods when China was invaded or occupied by foreign powers. Historical figures and real events often appear in his stories and are intertwined with the fictional plot. Heroism and patriotism are always the themes of his works. Many of his protagonists, such as Guo Jing in *The Legend of Condor Heroes* (《射雕英雄传》) and Zhang Wuji in *Heaven Sword and Dragon Saber* (《倚天屠龙记》), ②are courageous, selfless heroes who bravely fight against foreign invasion or rebel against the ruthless ruling of the Mongolian government.

His works also show respect for traditional Chinese values such as dignity, loyalty and honesty. But at the same time, Jin Yong questions the validity of some of these values from the perspective of modern society. For example, ③Yang Guo's romantic relationship with Xiao Long Nü in *The Return of Condor Heroes* (《神雕侠侣》), which should be considered extremely unethical according to Confucian values, is highly praised and glorified by the author.

His works are not only popular among common readers, but also draw the attention from the academic circle. A great many papers have been written by scholars and university professors, discussing, analyzing and debating over the artistic values of his novels. Needless to say, Jin Yong should be regarded as one of the greatest literary figures in contemporary China. (525 words)

Difficult Sentences

① Most of his works, though fictional, are set in the real historical periods when China was invaded or occupied by foreign powers. Historical figures and real events often appear in his stories and are intertwined with the fictional plot.

他的大多数作品，虽属虚构，但其创作背景却都是真实的——以中国历史上饱受异族入侵或占领为背景。故事中的历史人物和真实事件常与虚构的情节交织在一起。

② ... are courageous, selfless heroes who bravely fight against foreign invasion or rebel against the ruthless ruling of the Mongolian government.

（故事主人公）通常是无私无畏的英雄人物，勇敢地抗击外族侵略或反抗元朝政府的残暴统治。

③ ... Yang Guo's romantic relationship with Xiao Long Nü in *The Return of Condor Heroes*,

which should be considered extremely unethical according to Confucian values, is highly praised and glorified by the author.

《神雕侠侣》中杨过和小龙女的爱情故事，按照传统儒家观点有悖伦常，但却受到作者的高度赞美和颂扬。

Text 2   White Deer Plain

The Dream of the Red Chamber, one of China's four great classical novels, written in the middle of the eighteenth century by Cao Xueqin, records the decline and fall of two wealthy aristocratic clans in Jinling through a dream-like tale that revolves around the unpredictability and inconstancy of life. *White Deer Plain*, published in 1993, serves as a counterpoint to the *Dream of Red Chamber*. ①While the classical novel follows urban aristocrats, *White Deer Plain* traces the vicissitudes of two wealthy farm families in Shaanxi; where *Dream of Red Chamber* is almost surreal, *White Deer Plain* appears as realistic as a history book. Both books, though, see the world as a stage, and see those on stage demonstrating power over those beneath them.

White Deer Plain was written by Chen Zhongshi (1942—2016), a Chinese writer who grew up in rural Xi'an, Shaanxi province. Shaanxi has a long and rich cultural tradition. Xi'an, the capital city of Shaanxi, is the eastern terminus of the ancient Silk Road to Europe and Africa. ②One of the cradles of Chinese civilization, it served as the capital for thirteen dynasties, beginning with the Zhou Dynasty in 1046 BC. Chen was deeply rooted in his native land's rich culture and tried throughout his career to paint a realistic picture of countryside life there. It took him a decade to do research work and another six years to complete writing the novel. First published in 1993, it was the winner of 1997 Mao Dun Literature Prize, the highest literature prize for novelists in China, and was adapted into a popular film in 2011.

In the epigraph to the book Chen quotes Balzac, who believed that "the novel is no less than the secret history of nations." Chen's intention is hence revealed as clear as day: to tell the "secret" history of the nation, at least the rural part of China that he knew. To a significant extent, he has succeeded. In 2002, due to its ultra-realistic rendering of Chinese history, the novel was listed as one of the must-reads for college students in China.

White Deer Plain is the story of two landowner families, Bai and Lu, over half a century and three generations, in a rural area called White Deer Plain, in Shaanxi, China. The story starts around 1900 and ends in the 1950s, the early years of the People's Republic of China. The characters witness all the major events that took place during that period of Chinese history. Bai Jiaxuan, the protagonist and patriarch of the Bai family, is burdened with the urgent mission to produce a son, so that his family's lineage would continue unbroken. ③When Jiaxuan's father was dying, he asked his son to get married as soon as he passed away, instead of mourning for three years as the custom requires, because, as Confucian teaching goes, "Of the three unfilial conducts, the worst is to have no male descendant." The book begins with the story of his seven marriages, one following the other in quick succession. The first six wives die without a single child. Jiaxuan stops with the seventh marriage when his wife at last gives birth to three sons and a daughter.

After that, Jiaxuan devoted himself to the care of the village shrine, the place of ancestral worship. He is steeped in Confucian teachings and follows them carefully in his daily conduct. When two of his sons reach school age, he starts a school for all the village boys to attend. ④He is portrayed as a paragon of Confucianism: upstanding, morally uncompromised, flawless in his conduct, and widely respected in his village. He is famous for being a benevolent and righteous landowner, who treats his farmhand like a brother. But for all his efforts to offer a moral example to his children, his firstborn son commits adultery and conspires to send a good person to his death. And for all his benevolence, when his beloved daughter rebels against his patriarchal rule, Jiaxuan would rather see her die than break the marriage that he has arranged for her. ⑤Lu Zilin, the patriarch of the Lu family and counterpoint to Bai Jiaxuan, is a villain with no moral compass, who exhibits no redeeming characteristics and dies of senile dementia. In contrast to the Bai's, both of Lu's two sons turn out to be young men of noble character.

The two wealthy families, Bais and Lus, battle openly and covertly, seeking dominance in the village. There is no class conflict in Chen's novel. The biggest conflicts are not between the haves and have-nots. The factor that differentiates people is not class, not economic status, but morality. Those who follow Confucian teachings, despite being landowners, are depicted as being good; those who deviate from these teachings appear irredeemably evil. In the end, however, the world under Chen's pen is as senseless as "a tale told by an idiot."

⑥*White Deer Plain* was written under the influence of at least three Chinese literary movements: literature of introspection, literature of the wounded, and root-searching literature.

Chen wrote *White Deer Plain* and its protagonist, Bai Jiaxuan, in the image of Confucian teaching, examining China's history and bearing witness to the victims of its violent past. Despite the cultural and historical dimensions of this novel, literary work is first and foremost the story of deeply human experiences. It seems to be the author saying clearly: there is no meaning in experience; nothing matters as much as being alive, watching events unfold, like watching folk operas on the stage of White Deer Plain. (928 words)

Difficult Sentences

① Where the classical novel follows urban aristocrats, *White Deer Plain* traces the vicissitudes of two wealthy farm families in Shaanxi; where *Dream of Red Chamber* is almost surreal, *White Deer plain* appears as realistic as a history book.

《红楼梦》这部古典小说讲述了城市贵族的故事，而《白鹿原》则追溯了陕西乡村两大富裕家族的沧桑变迁；红楼梦中多玄妙，白鹿原上尽写实。

② One of the cradles of Chinese civilization, it served as the capital for thirteen dynasties, beginning with the Zhou Dynasty in 1046 BC.

西安是中华文明的摇篮，自公元前1046年的周朝始，曾为十三朝古都。

③ When Jiaxuan's father was dying, he asked his son to get married as soon as he passed away, instead of mourning for three years as the custom requires, because, as Confucian teaching goes, "Of the three unfilial conducts, the worst is to have no male descendant."

白嘉轩父亲去世前要求儿子在自己死后立刻娶妻，这不符合孝亲守丧三年的礼数，但遵循了儒家"不孝有三，无后为大"的教导。

④ He is portrayed as a paragon of Confucianism: upstanding, morally uncompromised, flawless in his conduct, and widely respected in his village.

他被描绘成儒家精神的典范代表：为人正直，道德上毫不妥协，行为上无懈可击，在村里备受尊重。

⑤ Lu Zilin, the patriarch of the Lu family and counterpoint to Bai Jiaxuan, is a villain with no moral compass, who exhibits no redeeming characteristics and dies of senile dementia.

鹿子霖是鹿家的族长，也是白嘉轩的对立面，他是个没有道德底线的反派，没有表现出任何值得嘉许的特点，最终死于老年痴呆。

⑥ *White Deer Plain* was written under the influence of at least three Chinese literary movements: literature of introspection, literature of the wounded, and root-searching literature.

《白鹿原》受到了至少三种中国现代文艺思潮的影响：即反思文学、伤痕文学和寻根文学。

Exercises 1

Task 1 Short Answer Questions

Directions: Read Text 1 and Text 2 and then answer the following questions briefly.

1. How are Jin Yong's "Wuxia" novels received by readers in Chinese-speaking regions?
2. What are the common themes of Jin Yong's books?
3. What characteristics do heroes in Jin Yong's works share?
4. What is Chen Zhongshi's intention in writing *White Deer Plain*?
5. What literary movements have impacted Chen when he wrote the novel?

Task 2 Reading Comprehension

Section A

Directions: *In this section, there are 5 incomplete sentences. You are required to select one word for each blank from a list of choices given in the word bank below. You may not use any of the words in the bank more than once.*

| chivalry | adapt | fictional | intertwine | validity |
| glorify | academic | released | contemporary | circumstance |

1. Yet in this terrible _____, there was no way to know what would happen next.

2. It is a serious crime to _____ the shameful past of a person as well as that of a nation.

3. The news should be _____ before 5 a.m. tomorrow.

4. _____ characters in novels or movies exert great influence on people in the real life.

5. Many scientists questioned the _____ of the findings of the experiment conducted by Professor Smith.

Section B

Directions: *Match the sentences in Column A with the corresponding interpretations in Column B.*

Column A	Column B
1. Jin Yong questions the validity of some of these values from the perspective of modern society.	A. He was deeply influenced by the teachings of Confucianism and carefully observed them in his daily behavior.
2. Chen was deeply rooted in his native land's rich culture and tried throughout his career to paint a realistic picture of countryside life there.	B. It is not class, not economic status, but morality that distinguishes people.
3. He is steeped in Confucian teaching and follows it carefully in his daily conduct.	C. Deeply rooted in the rich culture of his hometown, Chen tried to portray the reality of village life there throughout his career.
4. The factor that differentiates people is not class, not economic status, but morality.	D. Jin Yong hasn't published any work in the past 40 years. But his books written 40 years ago are still popular now.
5. Now 40 years after his announcement of ceasing writing, his works are still on the best-seller list of book stores in China.	E. Jin Yong makes readers doubt whether some of these values are still true in the modern society.

Answers: 1-( ) 2-( ) 3-( ) 4-( ) 5-( )

Task 3 Translation

Directions: *Translate the following passage from Chinese into English.*

如今，阅读中国网络文学已成为不少海外读者的日常"打卡项"。中国网络文学品类丰富，展示出了多样化、精品化的创作特点，有超过半数读者认为中国网络文学与海外文学相比最大的优点就是内容更加充满想象力。与此同时，围绕网络文学IP进行改编的影视作品先后于国外获奖，使得中国网络文学IP影响力覆盖到更大的接受群体，开始反哺文学作品本身。

Task 4 Writing

Directions: *The recent three decades after 1978 have witnessed the booming of literature, music, film and other forms of art in China. Write an essay about a famous person in the circle of art. You should tell the readers who s/he is and introduce at least one representative piece of his/her works.*

Section B Listening and Speaking

Text 3 Situational Dialogue: An Interview of Liu Cixin

Upon the success of the first China's hard sci-fi film *The Wandering Earth*, the original story writer of this film and renowned sci-fi novelist Liu Cixin was interviewed.

Q: Science fiction is a comprehensive genre varying from time travel, aliens, space exploration to cyberpunk[1]. What is your genre of fascination?

Liu: We mentioned Arthur C. Clarke backstage. It's his work that guided me onto the path of making science fiction. ①What interested me most was the setting in his works, some faraway land, worlds so vast and unknown that we can only reach them through our imagination, the distant universe. It's those works with broad visions and in-depth space and time that sparked my interest.

Q: Does it have anything to do with your engineering background?

Liu: Not really. Engineering is more focused on reality, on craftsmanship. But what fascinates me most about sci-fi creation is the unknown, the future. It is a more transcending and philosophical idea. I actually wanted to study astrophysics, but my scores for the college entrance exam were not high enough. I could only get into an engineering college as the score requirement for the colleges with astrophysics departments are usually very high.

Q: What is a good relationship between literary sources and sci-fi films?

Liu: I feel like science fiction movies, especially high-budget sci-fi films are more suitable for original screenplays, but not adaptations. But in recent years, the proportion of adapted American sci-fi films is getting larger, ones like *The Martian* or *Arrival* or *Annihilation*. As far as I know, the *Dune* will start filming in March. However, I think China should make more original sci-fi films. The problem is that we lack good sci-

---

1 赛博朋克是一种人工智能科幻流派和大胆美术风格，起源于威廉·吉布森的《神经浪游者》，是一种基于20世纪80年代科技文化水平对未来的幻想风格。

fi screenwriters in our country. This is an urgent problem to be dealt with in the development of science fiction movies, but it also takes time to cultivate and encourage more sci-fi screenwriters. During this year's spring festival, two costly sci-fi films hit the Chinese cinema and reached massive success. This is seen as an astounding beginning of Chinese sci-fi movies.

Q: There are rumors online that Amazon wants to adapt *Three-Body Problem* into a 10 or 20 episode series. Any idea if it's true?

Liu: I've heard of it, but I myself don't know if it's true. Regarding the film adaptation, I have an interesting story. The Hong Kong Science Fiction Association sent me a sci-fi magazine with a letter from Arthur Clark. Arthur Clark mentioned that he was busy adapting his novel *Rendezvous with Rama* to a movie. They're about to start filming. It was written back in the 1970's, but has yet to hit the screen, and there has been constant news of its adaptation. It is normal to take a long time for the adaption of the *Three-Body Problem*. ②It is a bit difficult for Chinese filmmakers to adapt in terms of story line and visual effects considering our current experience and abilities in this industry.

Q: There is hard sci-fi and soft sci-fi. Do you think it's better for China to start with soft sci-fi? And then come with hard sci-fi stories like *Three-Body Problem*.

Liu: Previously I wasn't sure about how Chinese audiences would react to these sci-fi films. It has been a mystery and I'm always curious. We found part of the answer this spring festival, and their reaction has been very pleasing. ③ I think the right path would be the prosperity of various genres of sci-fi stories, both traditional hard sci-fi as well as more literal and popular sci-fi. I don't want Chinese sci-fi creations to be constrained by some certain work or a certain type of genre. Of course, it's still too early to say, and there is still a long way for us to go. (635 words)

Difficult Sentences

① What interested me most was the setting in his works, some faraway land, worlds so vast and unknown that we can only reach them through our imagination, the distant universe.
我最感兴趣的是他作品中的背景，那些遥远的土地或宇宙、广阔的未知世界，只能通过想象力到达。

② It is a bit difficult for Chinese filmmakers to adapt in terms of story line and visual effects considering our current experience and abilities in this industry.
考虑到我们目前在这个行业的经验和能力，中国电影人在改编故事和呈现视觉效果方面是有困难的。

③ I think the right path would be the prosperity of various genres of sci-fi stories, both traditional hard sci-fi as well as more literal and popular sci-fi.
我认为正确的道路是各种类型科幻故事的繁荣，无论传统的硬科幻还是文学性更强的流行科幻都更多一点。

Text 4 A Talk on Chinese Literature in the 20th Century

Good morning, everyone. Today I'm going to talk about the development of Chinese literature in the 20th century.

Chinese literature in the last century is closely related to the political situation at that time. The first decade of the twentieth century witnessed the fall of the weakening Qing Empire. ①The overthrow of the monarchy and establishment of the Republic of China in 1911 sparked new hope. Intellectuals and other patriotic groups were excited about this political transformation. It was in this spirit of reform and renaissance that one group of intellectuals, led by an American-educated scholar, Hu Shi (Hu Shih), proposed a major new direction for Chinese literature and language in 1917. The new movement called for using the vernacular language as the written language. The movement quickly took root among the writers. Lu Xun, now considered the father of modern Chinese literature, wrote "A Madman's Diary" (《狂人日记》), the first short story written in the vernacular. ②Many of the writings of the period were modeled after Western writers, especially the Russians.

On May 4, 1919, students in Beijing protested violently against the poor performance of the Chinese representatives to the Versailles peace conference (凡尔赛和会，巴黎和会), which awarded the former German concessions of Shandong to Japan instead of returning them to China. Writers became more active in politics, ③many producing critical realist works with a strong social commentary. During the same period of time, thoughts of Marxism and Communism were introduced to China. Under the influence of Communism, many writers turned to the left, forming the "League of Leftist Writers" (左联), lead by Lu Xun. Although Lu Xun never formally joined the Communist Party, he has been considered a communist hero for his support of leftist ideas. Other famous writers, such as Mao Dun, also used their pens as tool to criticize the society and the Kuomintang government (国民党政府) and expressed their political aspirations to build a modernized, democratic country.

After the founding of the People's Republic of China in 1949, a new literary trend emerged under the guidance of Mao Zedong's "Talks on the Forum of Literature and Art in Yan'an" (《在延安文艺座谈会上的讲话》). Many writers began the creation of revolutionary, or proletarian literature, ④which should reflect the life of people in rural areas and be in the service of people, and in the service of revolution. Zhao Shuli is an outstanding representative of these writers. His most famous work, *The Marriage of Xiao Er Hei* (《小二黑结婚》), is written in a humorous tone and based on the local language of peasants at that time. The novel reflects the moral goodness of the oppressed peasants and the cruelty of the landlords, who stand for the dark old society.

With the end of the Cultural Revolution and the beginning of reform and opening up, literature and other forms of art in China entered a new phase of rapid development. Works of western literature, which were banned during the Cultural Revolution, now swarmed into book stores in China, while many talented Chinese writers made themselves well-known nationwide through their creative, experimental novels and poems. Among them, the most famous must be Mo Yan, who wins the Nobel Prize for Literature in 2012. The Nobel literature laureate, "⑤who with hallucinatory realism merges folk tales, history and the contemporary," is now regarded as a national hero and his success is inspiring the younger generation of Chinese writers, bringing them encouragement and confidence. Chinese literature is showing vitality and dynamism in a new era. (634 words)

Difficult Sentences

① The overthrow of the monarchy and establishment of the Republic of China in 1911 sparked new hope.
1911年君主制的推翻和中华民国的建立燃起了新的希望。

② were modeled after: 模仿，以……为模板

③ many producing critical realist works with a strong social commentary
带有社会评论性的批判现实主义作品

④ which should reflect the life of people in rural areas and be in the service of people, and in the service of revolution
（这些作品）应该反映广大农民的生活，并且要为人民服务，为革命服务

⑤ who with hallucinatory realism merges folk tales, history and the contemporary
他把魔幻现实主义与民间故事、历史和当代社会融合在一起

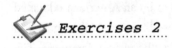
Exercises 2

Task 1 Listening Comprehension

Directions: Listen to the Dialogue in Text 3 and read the four choices marked A, B, C and D and decide which is the best answer.

1. Which sci-fi author influenced Liu Cixin the most?
    A. Jules Verne.   B. Asimov.   C. Arthur Clarke.   D. Ye Yonglie.
2. What is the difference between engineering and sci-fi according to Liu?
    A. Engineering focuses on reality whereas sci-fi cares more about the unknown.
    B. Engineering is about craftsmanship whereas sci-fi is about friendship.
    C. Engineering demands knowledge whereas sci-fi requires imagination.
    D. Engineering is hard whereas sci-fi is easy to understand.
3. What is the urgent problem to be dealt with in the development of science fiction movies in our country?
    A. The inefficiency of film-making process.
    B. The lack of good sci-fi screenwriters.
    C. The tightness of film-making budgets.
    D. The indifference of common audience.

4. What is Liu Cixin's idea upon the adaptation of his novel *Three-Body Problem*?

    A. There is a long way to go before it hits the screen.

    B. The novel will be adapted by Chinese filmmakers.

    C. The novel will be adapted by Hollywood filmmakers.

    D. There will be an adaptation along with Clarke's work.

5. What is the right path to develop Chinese sci-fi?

    A. To encourage hard sci-fi only.

    B. To encourage popular sci-fi only.

    C. To encourage film adaptations.

    D. To encourage all sorts of genres of sci-fi stories.

Task 2 Spot Dictation

Directions: *You will hear the passage based on Text 4 three times. When the passage is read for the first time, you should listen carefully of its general idea. When the passage is read for the second time, you are required to fill in the blanks with the exact words you have just heard. Finally, when the passage is read for the third time, you should check what you have written.*

Chinese literature in the last century is (1)_____ the political situation at that time. The first decade of the twentieth century (2)_____ the fall of the weakening Qing Empire. The overthrow of the monarchy and establishment of the Republic of China in 1911 sparked new hope. Intellectuals and other patriotic groups were excited about this political (3)_____. It was in this spirit of reform and renaissance that one group of (4)_____, led by an American-educated scholar, Hu Shi (Hu Shih), proposed a major new direction for Chinese literature and language in 1917. The new movement called for using the vernacular language as the written language. The movement quickly (5)_____ among the writers. Lu Xun, now considered the father of modern Chinese literature, wrote "A Madman's Diary," the first short story written in vernacular. Many of the writings of the period were modeled after Western writers, especially the Russians.

With the end of the Cultural Revolution and the beginning of reform and opening up, literature and other forms of art in China (6)_____ a new phase of rapid development. Works of western literature, which were (7)_____ during the Cultural Revolution, now swarmed into book stores in China, while many (8)_____ Chinese writers made themselves well-known nationwide through their creative, experimental novels and poems. Among them, the most famous must be Mo Yan, who won the Nobel Prize for Literature in 2012. The Nobel literature laureate, "who with hallucinatory realism merges folk tales, history and the contemporary," is now (9)_____ as a national hero and his success is (10)_____ the younger generation of Chinese writers, bringing them encouragement and confidence. Chinese literature is showing vitality and dynamism in a new era.

Task 3 Short Answer Questions

Directions: *Read Text 4 and answer in brief the following questions.*

1. What did the literary movement led by Hu Shi and other scholars call for?
2. What change did the May Fourth Movement bring about to Chinese writers at that time?
3. What thoughts were introduced from Russia to China?
4. What is the theme of the novel *The Marriage of Xiao Er Hei*?
5. How does Mo Yan, the Nobel Prize winner, influence the young Chinese writers?

Task 4 Translation

Directions: *Translate the following passage from Chinese into English.*

莫言出生于山东省一个农民家庭。他是中国第一位获得诺贝尔文学奖的作家,同时也是当代中国最负盛誉的小说家之一。在他的作品里,想象(fantasy)和现实、过去和现在常常彼此交织在一起。这些小说深刻地反映了中国农民的处境以及农村的发展和变化。莫言的一些作品还被改编成电影,这些电影同样获得了巨大的成功,并在各种电影节里获奖。

Words and Expressions Related to Literature

Text 1	
bootleg copies	盗版
couplet	*n.* 对联
protagonist	*n.* 主人公
Text 2	
counterpoint	*n.* 对比物
unpredictability	*n.* 不可预知
vicissitude	*n.* 变迁
epigraph	*n.* 题词
landowner	*n.* 地主
lineage	*n.* 香火
benevolent	*adj.* 仁慈的
farmhand	*n.* 佃农
conspire	*v.* 密谋
covertly	*adv.* 暗地里
aristocratic	*adj.* 贵族的
inconstancy	*n.* 变化无常
terminus	*n.* 终点
ultra-realistic	*adj.* 超现实主义的
senile dementia	老年性痴呆

续表

patriarch	*n.* 族长
paragon	*n.* 典范
righteous	*adj.* 正直的
adultery	*n.* 通奸
irredeemably	*adv.* 不可救药地
transcending	*adj.* 超验的
Text 3	
craftsmanship	*n.* 工匠精神
astrophysics	*n.* 天体物理学
cyberpunk	*adj. / n.* 赛博朋克
Text 4	
renaissance	*n.* 复兴
concessions	*n.* 特权
proletarian	*n.* 无产阶级
vernacular language	白话

Unit 3 Chinese Language and Literature

Key to Exercises

Before You Start

1. Among Jin Yong's works, I like *The Legend of Condor Heroes* best and Guo Jing is my favorite character. Though he seems dumb and stupid, he is in fact very kind-hearted and courageous. He finally masters different schools of Kung Fu and becomes the most skillful and powerful man at that time. Moreover, he struggles vigorously against the Mongolian rulers. His heroic deeds symbolize the traditional Chinese virtues of honor, loyalty and courage.
2. It's "A Madman's Diary" (《狂人日记》). The story alleges to be a dairy written by a "madman." After reading extensively the Chinese classics, he saw the words "eating people" between the lines. The story attacks the harmful effect of feudal values on the Chinese nation.

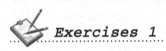

Exercises 1

Task 1 Short Answer Questions

1. His "Wuxia" works enjoy a widespread popularity in Chinese-speaking regions.

2. Heroism and patriotism are always the themes of his novels.

3. Many of his protagonists are courageous and selfless heroes.

4. Chen Zhongshi's intention is to write the history of a nation, at least the part he is familiar with.

5. Three movements: literature of introspection, literature of the wounded, and root-searching literature.

Task 2 Reading Comprehension

Part A

1. circumstance   2. glorify   3. released   4. Fictional   5. validity

Part B

1—E   2—C   3—A   4—B   5—D

Task 3 Translation

Nowadays, reading Chinese online literature has become a daily "punch line" for many overseas readers. More than half of the readers think that the biggest advantage of Chinese online literature compared with overseas literature is that the content is more imaginative. At the same time, the film and television works adapted around the IP of online literature have won awards abroad, making the influence of Chinese online literature IP reach a larger group of receivers and begin to feed the literary works themselves. Meanwhile, films and TV series adapted or based on those famous online literary works had won awards around the world. The Chinese online literature is reaching a larger group of audience as a result, affecting the mainstream literature in turn.

Task 4 Writing
Sample Writing
Yu Hua was born in 1960 in Zhejiang province of southeastern China. He used to be a dentist, but came to public notice as a writer of experimental fiction in the late 1980s. Later he became a professional writer. Yu was first known by the public through his short stories such as "On the Road at 18" (《十八岁出门远行》). These stories are marked by the unique style and content. The calm, indifferent depiction of violence and other controversial topics as well as the experimental language attracts a lot of readers but also arouses heated debates among them.

The most frequently mentioned work of his is *To Live* (《活着》). In writing this fiction, he gives up his usual experimental way but returns to traditional storytelling. By recording nearly the whole life of the protagonist Fu Gui, the novel vividly depicts the social transformation in the past half century as well as many aspects of the life of Chinese people during this process. (175 words)

Exercises 2

Task 1 Listening Comprehension
1. C   2. A   3. B   4. A   5. D

Task 2 Spot Dictation
1. closely related to   2. witnessed   3. transformation   4. intellectuals   5. took root
6. entered   7. banned   8. talented   9. is now regarded as   10. inspiring

Task 3 Short Answer Questions
1. The use of vernacular language
2. Many of them became more active in politics.
3. Thoughts of Marxism and Communism
4. The novel reflects the moral goodness of the peasants and the cruelty of the landlords.
5. His success is inspiring and encouraging the young generation of Chinese writers.

Task 4 Translation
Mo Yan was born into a peasant family in Shandong province. He is the first Chinese writer to win the Nobel Prize for Literature and one of the most acclaimed contemporary Chinese

novelists. Fantasy and reality, past and present are often intertwined with each other in his works. These novels profoundly reflect the situation of Chinese peasants and the development and changes in the countryside. Some of Mo Yan's works have also been adapted into films, which have also been highly successful and have won awards in various film festivals.

Unit 4 Chinese Education

导 读

本单元旨在介绍当代中国教育的现状，帮助学生更好地了解中国教育的改革和发展，以便学生能运用相关背景知识和英语表达方式进行跨文化交流，向世界展示中国当代教育的特点。

Before You Start

While you are preparing for this unit, think about the following questions:
1. What do you think is the major achievement of Chinese education and which educational area needs urgent improvement?
2. Do you still remember the day when you took college entrance exam? Some people say this standardized test guarantees equal opportunity to everyone, while others question it as the sole determinant for college admission. What's your opinion?

Section A Reading and Writing

Text 1 Reforming Chinese Education

① China's rapid economic growth has been fueled by low-skilled cheap labor. But with the aging population and rising labor costs, it is likely that a transition away from a low-end, labor-intensive manufacturing economy towards a knowledge-based service one is of primary importance to the country, and it significantly increases the relative value of education. Government should increase investment in education, develop world-class universities and improve the overall quality of education.

The famous rocket scientist Qian Xuesen once stated that China has not fully developed a university capable of following a model that can produce creative and innovative talents; none has its own unique innovations, and thus has not produced distinguished individuals. Distinguished individuals' are not ordinary talents, but truly distinguished masters. Nowadays the college student population has been on the rise and our universities are getting larger, but how to prepare more distinguished talents is still an impending (迫在眉睫的) issue.

We have plenty of reasons to be anxious and concerned over the shortage of innovations. ② Despite China's astounding double-digit growth for more than two decades, it was not innovation that drive the dramatic advancement that has unfolded in China, during which some 700 million people have been raised—or lifted themselves—out of desperate poverty. Instead the real driver has in large part been what might be a seemingly limitless supply of cheap labor. China devoted itself to the massive production of innovations, among which only a small number was innovated in China. Although billions of dollars' worth of products are made in China, however, they are not created by China.

Furthermore, an economy built on low-wage labor is very volatile (不稳定的) when there are plenty of other alternatives out there. According to a report from the U.S National Bureau of Economic Research, China's share of world exports for labor-intensive goods reached their height in 2013 at 39.3% and declined to 31.6% by 2018. Given factors such as the rise of labor costs and the shrink of work force, the so-called "the world's factory" is slowly losing its market share to newly emerging export economies in Asia, namely India, Bangladesh, Cambodia, Pakistan, and Vietnam.

③ The assessment of China's shortage of innovation stands at odds with its apparent progress in education. ④ Over the decades, China has been endeavoring to guarantee all school-age children the right to receive a minimum of nine years of education, known as nine-year compulsory education. China presently operates the world's largest formal education system, with a total student population of nearly 250 million, with about 52 million at the post-secondary level. Tertiary education in China has experienced a huge expansion in the 21st century. By 2020, the number of undergraduate students increased to more than 200 million from just over one million in 1980, and the number of graduate (master's and doctoral) students grew 50-fold over the same period.

⑤ Some educators have come to the conclusion that China's outstanding academic success, as indicated by test scores, may be what is holding it back. Now, China is searching for better education models elsewhere. Recent education reforms seek to foster innovation and entrepreneurship. They include relaxing central control of the curriculum, retraining teachers, reducing student academic load, and broadening college admissions criteria beyond test results.

In addition, ⑥ it is recommended that we should optimize the allocation of education resources, extend the period of compulsory education, promote the balanced development of education, develop high school as well as vocational and technical education, strengthen the training of on-the-job staff and train laborers to cope with the changing nature of industry and continually further their education. (616 words)

Difficult Sentences

① China's rapid economic growth has been fueled by low-skilled cheap labor.
低技能的廉价劳动力推动了中国经济的飞速发展。

② Despite China's astounding double-digit growth for more than two decades, it was not innovation that drive the dramatic advancement that has unfolded in China, during which some 700 million people have been raised—or lifted themselves—out of desperate poverty.
过去二十多年间,中国经济一直以惊人的两位数的速度增长。这期间,至少有7亿中国人民的生活得到了改善和提升,并实现了全社会脱贫,但是推动中国经济发展的重要力量并不是创新。

③ The assessment of China's shortage of innovation stands at odds with its apparent progress in education.
认为中国缺乏创新的评价与其在教育领域所取得的显著进步相互矛盾。

④ Over the decades, China has been endeavoring to guarantee all school-age children the right to receive a minimum of nine years of education, known as nine-year compulsory education.
近几十年,中国一直致力于保障所有适龄儿童都能至少能接受九年的教育,也称作九年义务教育。

⑤ Some educators have come to the conclusion that China's outstanding academic success, as indicated by test scores, may be what is holding it back.
有些教育家得出结论说,以考试成绩作为衡量学术成就的标准可能已经成为中国取得学术成就的羁绊。

⑥ it is recommended that we should optimize the allocation of education resources
有建议提出,我们必须优化教育资源配置

Text 2 Online Education: Ushering in a New Era of China's Education

COVID-19 has exerted its great impact on education worldwide, leading to the near-total closures of schools, universities and colleges. Nearly 1.5 billion children and young people around the world were badly affected by the crisis. This includes a total of 282 million Chinese students who were unable to start their spring semester (February – August 2020) on campus as planned. To minimize the impact on continuity of education, the Chinese Government has required all schools and higher education institutions across the country to use online delivery as an alternative to face-to-face teaching. ① Of significance, this marks the large scale of online delivery has been permitted as part of formal education delivery in China.

To support education institutions' transition to online learning, efforts have been made by the Ministry of Education (MoE) to provide uninterrupted learning for students affected by the ongoing pandemic. The authority requested schools at various levels to use online platforms to facilitate remote study and recommended a list of online platforms capable of providing online courses for free.

These materials include MOOCs (Massive Open Online Courses), SPOCs (Small Private Online Courses) and virtual simulation experiments covering 12 disciplines at undergraduate level and 18 disciplines at higher vocational level. The majority of platforms listed by the MoE, especially MOOCs, are established by top Chinese universities or for-profit educational enterprises, offering a wide range of courses across a variety of disciplines. More than half of China's higher education institutions commenced the spring semester online using MOOC platforms and live-streamed classes, with 1.08 million teachers producing 1.1 million online courses. ② The innovative integration of online education and MOOCs have been leveraged to promote educational equity and sharing of quality educational resources so that everyone can learn whenever and wherever they want.

At the school level, to help primary and secondary school students continue their studies at home, the MoE has decided to open a "National Online Cloud Classroom" (www.eduyun.cn), an online learning platform providing digital materials for schools to conduct teaching online and is capable of supporting 50 million students using it simultaneously. An MoE official explained: ③ "Whilst classes may be suspended, there is no reason to suspend teaching or learning. A cloud-based classroom has therefore been set up to help children study at home." As of 11 May 2020, the platform had been visited over 2 billion times by people from China.

However, with online lessons replacing classrooms, the MoE also noted that students in villages and poorer regions were disproportionately affected by the new study conditions. Many students with limited access to technology and the internet agree that their learning has been affected. "I don't have a laptop and have to use my phone for online classes," confirms a student in rural Hubei. "Sometimes, the connection would break, so I would go on the rooftop to follow the lecture." To cater to the needs of such students, the ministry urged local communication departments and basic telecom operators to strengthen network coverage and implement preferential measures for impoverished students to ease their pressure of internet charges.

As the COVID-19 situation stabilized in China, schools are now open up to students. ④In this situation, the education sector of China will leverage the strengths of online education platforms to build a more flexible, easily accessible, rich-in-content system of lifelong high-quality educational learning where learning happens everywhere, anytime, for everyone.

In order to promote the high-quality development of China's overall education system, China plans to significantly improve its online education system. It is said that by 2025, China will establish an interconnected system of online education platforms and a comprehensive

resource pool of online courses, covering all subjects and all versions of textbooks. In addition, China will have a full set of policies implemented to support the operation and development of online education. It has also emphasized the building of online education platforms from national-level to school-level, so as to ensure that online education resources are accessible to all students. (671 words)

 Difficult Sentences

① Of significance, this marks the large scale of online delivery has been permitted as part of formal education delivery in China.
这标志着在中国大规模在线教育已被允许作为正规教育的一部分。

② The innovative integration of online education and MOOCs have been leveraged to promote educational equity and sharing of quality educational resources so that everyone can learn whenever and wherever they want.
慕课和在线教育的创新性融合，推动了教育公平及优质教育资源共享，从而实现人人皆学、处处能学、时时可学。

③ "Whilst classes may be suspended, there is no reason to suspend teaching or learning. A cloud-based classroom has therefore been set up to help children study at home."
"线下停课并不意味着停教或停学。既然如此，我们就搭建云课堂，让孩子们也能在家开展学习。"

④ In this situation, the education sector of China will leverage the strengths of online education platforms to build a more flexible, easily accessible, rich-in-content system of lifelong high-quality educational learning where learning happens everywhere, anytime, for everyone.
在当前形势下，中国的教育行业将借助在线教育平台的优势，构建一个更灵活、更便捷、内容更丰富的终身优质教育学习体系，让教育无处不在，学习随时随地。

 Exercises 1

Task 1 Short Answer Questions

Directions: *Read Text 1 and Text 2 and then answer the following questions briefly.*

1. What should our government do to quickly transform from a low-end, labor-intensive manufacturing economy into one based on knowledge?
2. What have threatened China's status as the "world's factory"?
3. What do recent education reforms seek to do?
4. What has the government done for the underprivileged children during their online learning?

5. Why is China eager to take all measures to support the operation and development of online education?

Task 2 Reading Comprehension

Part A

Directions: *Complete the following five sentences with the proper forms of the words given in the brackets.*

1. We have plenty of reasons to be anxious and concerned over the _____ (short) of innovations.

2. Tertiary education in China experienced a huge _____ (expand) in the 21st century.

3. They include relaxing central control of the curriculum, retraining teachers, reducing student _____ (academy) load, and broadening college admissions criteria beyond test results.

4. To minimize the impact on continuity of education, the Chinese government has required all schools and higher education institutions across the country to use online delivery as an _____ (alter) to face-to-face teaching.

5. The majority of platforms listed by the MoE, especially MOOCs, are established by top Chinese universities or for-profit educational enterprises, _____ (offer) a wide range of courses across a variety of disciplines.

Part B

Directions: *Match the sentences in Column A with the corresponding interpretations in Column B.*

Column A	Column B
It is likely that a transition away from a low-end, labor-intensive manufacturing economy towards a knowledge-based service one is of primary importance, and it significantly increases the relative value of education.	A. Despite the fact that we now have more college students and larger universities, there is still a very urgent question facing us: how to foster more distinguished talents?
2. Nowadays the college student population has been on the rise and our universities are getting larger, but how to prepare more distinguished talents is still an impending issue.	B. Educational institutions and schools nationwide were urged by the authorities to shift from offline to online courses.
3. The innovative integration of online education and MOOCs have been leveraged to promote educational equity and sharing of quality educational resources so that everyone can learn whenever and wherever they want.	C. To convert China's economy from a labor intensive one into a knowledge intensive one, education is a key aspect to be involved.
4. The government has required all schools and higher education institutions across the country to use online delivery as an alternative to face-to-face teaching.	D. The groundbreaking collaboration between online learning and open-source educational platforms have seen some positive results.

Answers: 1-( ) 2-( ) 3-( ) 4-( )

Task 3 Translation

Directions: *Translate the following passage from Chinese into English.*

教育部称，截至今年8月，我国慕课学习人数约达2.7亿。目前慕课数量约1.5万门，我国已建成涵盖多个学科、内容广泛的慕课网络。在慕课学习者中，约有8000万人为高校学生。慕课网络平台为教育公平作出了巨大的贡献。在教育部组织的几项计划中，多所西部欠发达地区的高校试图在其课程中引入在线开放课程，并就整合线上线下课程对教职员工进行培训。截至目前，西部高校引入线上教学或线上线下课程8000多门，接受培训教师达5.2万人次。教育部还计划于今年年底前推出中国慕课双语门户网站，以连接国内约20个慕课网站。

Task 4 Writing

Directions: *What do you think a world-class university is supposed to be like? Then write a composition on* **My Ideal University**.

Section B   Listening and Speaking

Text 3 Situational Dialogue: China's Education

(A: Peter   B: Xiao Wang)

A: Hello, Xiao Wang. You know, in order to support my travelling fee in China, I want to find a job as an English teacher. Anyhow, I got a Bachelor's degree of Education two years ago in the U.S.A.

B: That's a good idea, Peter. I'm quite sure that will be a wonderful experience. What can I do to help you?

A: Yes, I do need your help. Could you please tell me something about China's education? Are there any differences?

B: ① Most Westerners naturally assume that what they will encounter in China is a model of education that is more or less similar to their own, barring a few cultural differences. But they will eventually find out that is not the case.

A: Oh? What's the fact?

B: ② What they find instead is a unique mixture of Confucian tradition and current political agenda interspersed with Western influence and a population of quite different students as well. All of these are nearly impossible for any foreigner to understand without having actually lived and taught here.

A: Can you tell me some differences in brief?

B: Ok. Our educational system is quite different. In China, we have the so-called *The Law on Nine-Year Compulsory Education*. According to this law, all citizens must attend school for at least nine years, six years of primary education and three years of secondary education in junior middle school.

A: That's great. It's well known that China is the most populous country in the world. So it's really not very easy to get all the people educated.

B: Yes. Our government has done a great deal of work to make sure that almost all the people can receive considerable education.

A: Then after 9 years of compulsory education, what do people usually do if they want to be further educated?

B: National entrance exams are required for admission into senior middle school and university, which are usually called Zhongkao and Gaokao respectively.

A: I have heard a lot about Gaokao. Can you tell me more about it?

B: ③ Gaokao, literally meaning "tall exam," is an informal abbreviation for China's National College Entrance Exam, often explained—tongue-in-cheek—that it is so abbreviated because it looms so large in the lives of all Chinese.

A: Just now you told me the Chinese students are also very different. How about that?

B: Although at the same age, the Chinese students are quite different from the American students. Considering the different environment between the two groups, you can easily find out the reasons which caused these great differences in their daily lives. There is no clear answer to the question that who is better, but maybe it is clear that the Chinese students feel more pressure than the American students at the same age.

A: You told me some differences that I didn't know. It seems I have a lot to learn if I want to be a teacher in China.

B: Of course.

(506 words)

Difficult Sentences

① Most Westerners naturally assume that what they will encounter in China is a model of education that is more or less similar to their own, barring a few cultural differences.
大部分西方人想当然地认为，除了一些文化上的差异，他们在中国见到的教育体制和自己国家的教育体制将会相差无几。

② What they find instead is a unique mixture of Confucian tradition and current political agenda interspersed with Western influence and a population of quite different students as well.
然而，实际上他们发现这是一个既有儒家传统又有当代政治特色，还受到西方影响，同时具备独特学生群体的综合体。

③ Gaokao, literally meaning "tall exam," is an informal abbreviation for China's National College Entrance Exam, often explained—tongue-in-cheek—that it is so abbreviated because it looms so large in the lives of all Chinese.
高考在字面上的意思为"很高的考试"，它是高等学校招生全国统一考试的非正式简称。中国人会半开玩笑地解释说，高考之所以得名是因为它对所有中国人生活的影响实在是太大了。

Text 4 Tao Xingzhi

Tao Xingzhi (1891—1946) is one of China's highest-profile educationists. In 1914, he graduated from the Department of Literature of Jinling University in Nanjing. After that, he studied Political Science at the University of Illinois and then Education at Columbia University in the United States. Since 1917 when he returned to China, he served as a professor in Nanjing Higher Normal School and dean of the Department of Education of Southeast University. Successively, he initiated Chinese Association for the Promotion of Civilian Education in 1923, Xiaozhuang Normal School in Nanjing in 1927, Yucai School in Chongqing in 1939, and Social University in Chongqing in 1946. Unfortunately, he died of cerebral hemorrhage in Shanghai on July 25, 1946.

① His major works include *China's Educational Reform, Universal Education, Bell Ringing in Ancient Temple, Xingzhi Collected Letters* and so on. In 1984, *Tao Xingzhi Collected Works* were published by Hunan Education Publishing House. The creation of Chinese Society for Tao Xingzhi Studies in 1985 marked a new milestone of the studies on his educational theories and thoughts. The wealth of his educational theories and thoughts has become a valuable resource in the history of Chinese education.

Tao Xingzhi's Educational Mottos:

1. Life Education

② Basic viewpoints of life education are "Life as Education," "Society as School" and "Unity of Teaching, Learning and Reflective Acting."

1) "Life as Education." ③ "Learning begins at birth and ends at death." "A good life means a good education. On the contrary, a bad life means a bad education."

2) "Society as School." ④ "It is to free the caged birds to soar in the sky, and to extend everything in the school into nature."

3) "Unity of Teaching, Learning and Reflective Acting." ⑤ "Teaching, Learning and Reflective Acting is one thing, not three things. We must teach by reflective acting and learn by reflective acting. It is a teacher who teaches by reflective acting; it is a student who learns by reflective acting. From the perspective of the teacher, reflective acting is teaching; from the perspective of the students, reflective acting is learning. Teaching by reflective acting is true

teaching; learning by reflective acting is real learning. Without reflective acting, teaching is not the true teaching, and learning is not the real learning."

2. Creative Education

⑥ "Action is dad, thought son, and creation grandson. Without dad and son, there would be no grandson. This has always been the case." ⑦ "To create, you shall experiment with your hands while you use your brains; you think with your brains while you use your hands. Using both hands and brains is just the beginning of creative education; unity of hands and brains is the purpose of creative education."

3. Preschool Education

⑧ "Education shall start from infancy. Infants, like seedlings, must be cultivated properly before they flourish and grow; otherwise, the infants who have suffered from damage will find it hard to succeed even if they don't die young."

4. Moral Education

⑨ "Morality is foundation of being a man. In the absence of the foundation, anyone, regardless of knowledge and capability, is good-for-nothing; moreover, for those without morality, the greater the knowledge and capability, the greater the evil."

His educational thoughts are closely combined with practices. His educational theories come from practices and then guide practices. Currently, the studies concerning his educational theories and thoughts are still of great significance in China's educational reform. First, by combining education with life, students shall be encouraged to learn new knowledge in their practices and apply what they have learned into their real lives. Second, national progress and development can't thrive without creativity; therefore, we must spare no effort to cultivate students' creativity. Third, teachers shall teach students in accordance with their aptitudes and give corresponding education according to their diversified needs. ⑩ Fourth, students shall stress on both morality and capability dominated by the morality, and enhance cultivation of ideology and morality.

Tao Xingzhi dedicated himself to Chinese people' education. ⑪ "The purpose of teaching is to teach how to seek the truth, and learning to learn how to be a truth-seeker" is his educational motto. ⑫ "A good educator devotes to education without seeking social return" is just vivid portrayal of his life. (708 words)

Difficult Sentences

① His major works include *China's Educational Reform, Universal Education, Bell Ringing in Ancient Temple, Xingzhi Collected Letters* and so on. In 1984, *Tao Xingzhi Collected Works* were published by Hunan Education Publishing House.
他的主要著作有《中国教育改造》《普及教育》《古庙敲钟录》《行知书信集》等。1984年，湖南教育出版社出版《陶行知全集》。

② Basic viewpoints of life education are "Life as Education," "Society as School" and "Unity of Teaching, Learning and Reflective Acting."
生活教育的基本观点是"生活即教育""社会即学校""教学做合一"。

③ Learning begins at birth and ends at death. 出世便是破蒙，进棺材才算毕业。

④ It is to free the caged birds to soar in the sky, and to extend everything in the school into nature.
它是要把笼中的小鸟放到天空中，使它能任意翱翔，是要把学校的一切伸展到大自然里去。

⑤ Teaching, Learning and Reflective Acting is one thing, not three things. We must teach by reflective acting and learn by reflective acting. It is a teacher who teaches by reflective acting; it is a student who learns by reflective acting. From the perspective of the teacher, reflective acting is teaching; from the perspective of the students, reflective acting is learning. Teaching by reflective acting is true teaching; learning by reflective acting is real learning. Without reflective acting, teaching is not the true teaching, and learning is not the real learning.
教学做是一件事，不是三件事。我们要在做上教，在做上学。在做上教的是先生；在做上学的是学生。从先生对学生的关系来说：做便是教；从学生对先生的关系说：做便是学。先生拿做来教，乃是真教；学生拿做来学，方是实学。不在做上用功夫，教固不成为教，学也不成为学。

⑥ Action is dad, thought son, and creation grandson. Without dad and son, there would be no grandson. This has always been the case.
行动老子，思想是儿子，创造是孙子。你要有孙子，非先有老子、儿子不可，这是一贯下来的。

⑦ To create, you shall experiment with your hands while you use your brains; you think with your brains while you use your hands. Using both hands and brains is just the beginning of creative education; unity of hands and brains is the purpose of creative education.
要创造，非你在用脑的时候，同时用手去实验；用手的时候，同时用脑去想不可。手和脑一块儿干，是创造教育的开始；手脑双全，是创造教育的目的。

⑧ Education shall start from infancy. Infants, like seedlings, must be cultivated properly before they flourish and grow; otherwise, the infants who have suffered from damage will find it hard to succeed even if they don't die young.
教人要从小教起。幼儿比如幼苗，必须培养得宜，方能发芽滋长；否则幼年受到损伤，即不夭折，也难成材。

⑨ Morality is foundation of being a man. In the absence of the foundation, anyone, regardless of knowledge and capability, is good-for-nothing; moreover, for those without morality, the greater the knowledge and capability, the greater the evil.
道德是做人的根本。根本一坏，纵然你有一些学问和本领，也无甚用处，并且，没有道德的人，学问和本领愈大，就能为非作恶愈大。

⑩ Fourth, students shall stress on both morality and capability dominated by the morality, and enhance cultivation of ideology and morality.
第四，学生要以德为先，德才兼备，加强思想道德修养。

⑪ "The purpose of teaching is to teach how to seek the truth, and learning to learn how to be a truth-seeker" is his educational motto.

"千教万教，教人求真；千学万学，学做真人"是他的教育箴言。（此句中 learning to learn是the purpose of learning is to learn的省略。）

⑫ "A good educator devotes to education without seeking social return" is just vivid portrayal of his life.

"捧着一颗心来，不带半根草去"正是他一生的生动写照。

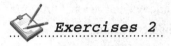

Exercises 2

Task 1 Listening Comprehension (Based on Text 3)

Directions: Listen to the Situational Dialogue in Text 3, read the four choices marked A, B, C and D, and decide which is the best answer.

1. What kind of job does Peter want to find in China?
   A. A translator.   B. An interpreter.   C. An English teacher.   D. A tourist guide.

2. Most Westerners take for granted that _____.
   A. China's education is quite the same to theirs
   B. China's education is totally different from theirs
   C. China's education is different from theirs in some way
   D. China's education is similar to theirs to some extent

3. According to Xiao Wang, China's education is a unique mixture of following different components EXCEPT _____.
   A. Confucius tradition
   B. Western influence
   C. a population of quite different students
   D. traditional political agenda

4. According to _____, all citizens must attend six years of primary education and three years of secondary education in junior middle school.
   A. The Constitution
   B. The Law on Nine-year Compulsory Education
   C. The Criminal Law
   D. The Education Law

5. Which of the following states is NOT true according to the conversation?
   A. For admission into senior middle school, students must attend Gaokao.
   B. Gaokao is an informal abbreviation for China's National College Entrance Exam.
   C. Gaokao is very important in the lives of Chinese people.
   D. Gaokao literally means "tall exam."

Task 2 Spot Dictation

Directions: *You will hear a passage based on Text 4 three times. When the passage is read for the first time, you should listen carefully for its general idea. When the passage is read for the second time, you are required to fill in the blanks with the exact words you have just heard. Finally, when the passage is read for the third time, you should check what you have written.*

1. Life Education

Basic viewpoints of life education are "Life as Education," "Society as School" and "Unity of Teaching, Learning and Reflective Acting."

1) "Life as Education." "Learning begins at (1) _____ and ends at death." "A good life means a good education. On the contrary, a bad life means a bad education."

2) "Society as School." "It is to free the caged birds to (2) _____ in the sky, and to (3) _____ everything in the school into nature."

3) "Unity of Teaching, Learning and Reflective Acting." "Teaching, Learning and Reflective Acting is one thing, not three things. We must teach by reflective acting and learn by reflective acting. It is a teacher who teaches by reflective acting; it is a student who learns by reflective acting. From the perspective of the teacher, reflective acting is teaching; from the perspective of the students, reflective acting is learning. Teaching by reflective acting is true teaching; learning by reflective acting is real learning. Without reflective acting, teaching is not the true teaching, and learning is not the real learning."

2. Creative Education

"Action is dad, thought son, and creation grandson. Without dad and son, there would be no grandson. This has always been the case." "To create, you shall (4) _____ with your hands while you use your brains; you think with your brains while you use your hands. Using both hands and brains is just the beginning of creative education; unity of hands and brains is the (5) _____ of creative education."

3. Preschool Education

"Education shall start from infancy. Infants, like (6) _____, must be cultivated properly before they (7) _____ and grow; otherwise, the infants who have suffered from (8) _____ will find it hard to succeed even if they don't die young."

4. Moral Education

"Morality is foundation of being a man. In the absence of the foundation, regardless of knowledge and (9) _____, anyone is good-for-nothing; moreover, for those without morality, the greater the knowledge and capability, the greater the (10) _____."

Task 3 Short Answer Questions

Directions: *Read Text 4 and answer in brief the following questions.*

1. Which schools did Tao Xingzhi found?
2. What is the significance of the creation of Chinese Society for Tao Xingzhi Studies?
3. What educational thoughts did Tao Xingzhi put forward?
4. What are the basic viewpoints of life education?
5. What is the purpose of creative education according to the text?

Task 4 Translation

Directions: *Translate the following passage from Chinese into English.*

陶行知是中国最著名的教育家之一。他先后创办了晓庄师范、育才学校和社会大学。1984年，湖南教育出版社出版《陶行知全集》。1985年9月5日，中国陶行知研究会在北京成立。陶行知提出了丰富的教育思想，如生活教育、创造教育、幼儿教育、德育等。生活教育是他教育思想体系的核心，其基本观点是"生活即教育""社会即学校""教学做合一"。陶行知毕生献身于中国人民的教育事业。"千教万教，教人求真；千学万学，学做真人"是他的教育箴言。"捧着一颗心来，不带半根草去"正是他一生的生动写照。

Words and Expressions for Chinese Education

Text 1	
indispensable	*adj.* 不可或缺的
world-class	*adj.* 世界级的
on the rise	在增加
double-digit growth	两位数的增长
labor/knowledge intensive	劳动/知识密集型
at odds with	与……意见不一致
on-the-job staff	在职员工
Text 2	
alternative	*adj.* 可替代的
pandemic	*n.* 大流行病
facilitate	*v.* 促进
simulation	*n.* 刺激
commence	*v.* 开始，着手做
live-steamed	*adj.* 直播的
innovative	*adj.* 革新的
leverage	*v.* 作为杠杆作用促使……改变
integration	*n.* 结合，整合
suspend	*v.* 延缓，延迟
replace	*v.* 替换
disproportionately	*adv.* 不均衡地
implement	*v.* 实施，贯彻，执行
impoverished	*adj.* 穷困的
comprehensive	*adj.* 综合的；详尽的
accessible	*adj.* 易得到的，易进入的

Text 3	
barring	prep. 不包括，除了
in brief	简而言之
tongue-in-cheek	adv. 半开玩笑地
loom	v. 隐约可见
Text 4	
highest-profile	adj. 最具知名度的，最受人瞩目的
educationist	n. 教育家，教育理论家
Jinling University in Nanjing	南京的金陵大学
the University of Illinois	伊利诺伊大学
political science	政治学
Columbia University	哥伦比亚大学
education	n. 教育学，教育
Nanjing Higher Normal School	南京高等师范学校
dean of Department of Education	教育系主任
Southeast University	东南大学
successively	adv. 先后，相继地，依次
initiate	v. 发起，创始
Chinese Association for the Promotion of Civilian Education	中华平民教育促进会
Xiaozhuang Normal School	晓庄师范
Yucai School	育才学校
Social University	社会大学
cerebral hemorrhage	脑溢血，脑出血
creation	n. 创建
Chinese Society for Tao Xingzhi Studies	中国陶行知研究会
milestone	n. 重要事件，里程碑
motto	n. 格言，箴言
reflective	adj. 沉思的，深思的
from the perspective of	从……的角度来看
brain	n. 头脑，脑力，智力
preschool	adj. 学（龄）前的 n. 幼儿园，学前班
infant	n. 幼儿
infancy	n. 幼儿期
seedling	n. 幼苗，秧苗
cultivate	v. 培养

续表

flourish	v. 茂盛，茁壮成长
moral	adj. 道德（上）的
morality	n. 道德
in the absence of	无……时，缺少……时
regardless of	不管，不顾
capability	n. 能力，才能
good-for-nothing	adj.（人）没用的，一无是处的
thrive	v. 兴旺发达，繁荣，蓬勃发展
spare no effort to do sth	不遗余力地做某事，竭尽全力地做某事
in accordance with	根据，按照
aptitude	n. 天资，天生的才能，天赋
corresponding	adj. 相应的
diversified	adj. 多样化的，各种的
dominated by	由……占主导地位，被……支配
enhance	v. 加强，提高
ideology	n. 思想意识，意识形态
dedicate oneself to sth / to doing sth	献（身）于
portrayal	n. 描绘，描写

Key to Exercises

Before You Start

1. The major educational achievement made by China education is the successful elimination of illiteracy, which should be considered as a great contribution to the national development and world civilization, for China has the largest population in the world. I think Chinese educational evaluation system needs urgent change. That is to say, we should shift our examination-oriented model to a quality-oriented one so as to better fit the demands of today's society.
2. Yes, definitely. It was considered to be the most miserable and stressful experience in my life, which I would certainly never forget. I think Gaokao should not be regarded as the sole determinant for college admission. Anyhow, we cannot judge a person by giving him/her only one chance.

Exercises 1

Task 1 Short Answer Questions

1. Our government should increase investment in education, develop world-class universities and improve the overall quality of education.

2. Rising labor costs and increasing value of its currency.

3. To foster innovation and entrepreneurship.

4. Preferential measures were taken for impoverished students to ease their pressure of internet charges.

5. In order to promote the high-quality development of China's education system.

Task 2 Reading Comprehension

Part A

1. shortage 2. expansion 3. academic 4. alternative 5. offering

Part B

1. C   2. A   3. D   4. B

Task 3 Translation

About 270 million people have taken massive open online courses (MOOC) in China as of August this year, according to the Ministry of Education. With around 15,000 courses, China has built an extensive MOOC network offering a wide range of courses across a variety of disciplines, said the ministry. Of the users, about 80 million were college students. The MOOC network has notably contributed to education equity, the ministry added. Under several programs sponsored by the ministry, colleges and universities in less-developed western regions have tried to introduce open online courses in their curriculums and trained their faculty in integrating online and offline courses. As of now, they have introduced more than 8,000 courses online or online-offline and 52,000 teachers have received the training. The ministry also plans to launch a bilingual gateway website of China MOOC by the end of this year to connect about 20 Chinese MOOC websites.

Task 4 Writing

My Ideal University

Tsinghua University has been my dream university since childhood, and I eventually achieved my dream through my hard working. With the time passing by, I figured out Tsinghua is really my ideal university.

First of all, I think Tsinghua is quite qualified as an ideal university for its teachers and facilities, which is an important factor of evaluating a university. Students can easily find a good studying atmosphere in well-equipped teaching buildings, libraries laboratories and with so many excellent teachers ready to help. Besides, I believe fellow schoolmates are even more important, for in the next 4 years, classmates are whom I will stay with for most of the time. Staying with top students helps me develop good study habits, increase my study efficiency, and meanwhile, make more friends, enlarging my social circle. Last but not least, Tsinghua offers undergraduate students high-quality living standards with low fees. Also, there is a famous saying in Tsinghua, "Work for homeland for 50 years healthily." To achieve this goal, Tsinghua provides students with enormous fields for sports. Many types of sports are available here, making our leisure time full of fun.

Someone may argue that compared with foreign universities Tsinghua is not that good in some fields. But there is no denying that the best is not always the most suitable one. In my case, I find Tsinghua more adaptive; as a result, Tsinghua is an ideal university to me. (240 words)

Exercises 2

Task 1 Listening Comprehension
1. C   2. D   3. D   4. B   5. A

Task 2 Spot Dictation
1. birth   2. soar   3. extend   4. experiment
5. purpose   6. seedlings   7. flourish   8. damage
9. capability   10. evil

Task 3 Short Answer Questions
1. Xiaozhuang Normal School, Yucai School and Social University.
2. It marked a new milestone of the studies on Tao Xingzhi's educational theories and thoughts.

3. Life education, creative education, preschool education, moral education, etc.

4. "Life as Education," "Society as School" and "Unity of Teaching, Learning and Reflective Acting."

5. Unity of hands and brains.

Task 4 Translation

Tao Xingzhi is one of China's highest-profile educationists. Successively, he initiated Xiaozhuang Normal School, Yucai School and Social University. In 1984, *Tao Xingzhi's Collected Works* were published by Hunan Education Publishing House. Chinese Society for Tao Xingzhi Studies was established in Beijing on September 5, 1985. Tao Xingzhi put forward abundant educational thoughts, such as life education, creative education, preschool education, moral education and so on. The life education is the core of his educational thought system, and its basic viewpoints are "Life as Education," "Society as School" and "Unity of Teaching, Learning and Reflective Acting." Tao Xingzhi dedicated himself to Chinese people's education. "The purpose of teaching is to teach how to seek the truth, and learning to learn how to be a truth-seeker" is his educational motto. "A good educator devotes to education without seeking social return" is just a vivid portrayal of his life.

Unit 5 Economy, Science and Technology

> **导 读**
>
> 本单元着重介绍中国古代"丝绸之路"的必经之地，今日西部改革开放窗口——喀什的发展及规划，并详细阐述了几项中国领先于世界的科技成就，如具有世界先进水平的深海潜水器"奋斗者"号和享有"世界之最"称号的中国青藏铁路。通过本单元内容的学习，学生能够了解中国的经济发展和科技进步，并运用所学中国文化知识及相关的英语表达进行跨文化交流。

Before You Start

While you are preparing for this unit, think about the following questions:
1. Do you know anything about Kashi, like its history, geographical location, climate or its important role in ancient Silk Road? After you have explored the above questions, think about what kind of role it will play in the future economic development in our country.
2. China has made rapid advances in science and technology in recent decades. Could you list a few fields that China is leading the world or has reached world level in science and technology?

Section A Reading and Writing

Text 1 A New Legend for an Ancient City

With the Silk Road's decline, Kashi's importance began to dwindle, a process that was accelerated by the emergence of China's coastal cities in the past 30 years of rapid national economic development.

Yet the city always dreamed of a renaissance. Today, with the Chinese government focusing on the development of the western regions, Kashi has a vital opportunity for rapid advancement.

In May 2010, a 50-sq-km Special Economic Zone was established in Kashi, the first inland economic development zone in China.

① Meanwhile, the southern coastal city of Shenzhen, the pioneer city in the reform and opening and the country's original Special Economic Zone, entered into a cooperation agreement with Kashi. The aim was to make Kashi an important window on the opening policy in western China and an economic growth point for the further development of Xinjiang Uygur autonomous region, and to build Kashi as a glorious pearl in western China that is admired in the neighboring countries and around the world.

However, the aim of the cooperation is not for Kashi to learn the development path of Shenzhen, but for it to learn its innovative spirit. Kashi, with its history, culture and its fragile ecological environment, couldn't copy Shenzhen's traditional development model, which involved the opening up of large areas of land, the quick expansion of industries and the building up of a significant population. Compared to Shenzhen's, Kashi's innovation should be an inland city's innovation. Shenzhen faces Hong Kong, a prosperous city; meanwhile, what Kashi faces are comparatively poorer neighboring regions, with behind it prosperous inland provinces and cities. Kashi has to find another way.

② On November 18, 2011, the Kashi government announced the "5th-generation new city" initiative. The core component of a 5th-generation city's development is reliance on the service economy, chiefly about finance, tourism and logistics, boosted by the values of low consumption and high output. The city will also recruit international experts who, without being required to live in the city, will contribute by making up for the shortage of local expertise in certain areas.

Nowadays, the local government is making great efforts to attain the target. Kashi's transport infrastructure is set to undergo a major improvement, aiming at making better use of the area's geographical advantages. New railways and highways connecting Kashi with the neighboring countries are planned to be built. Document No. 33 contains an explicit commitment to encouraging domestic and foreign airlines to establish air routes between Kashi and major cities and the neighboring countries. Ultimately, it is anticipated that a "Silk Road in the Sky" will be built.

Besides, the local government is making its own plans for creating a business boom. A comprehensive bonded area is about to be built in Kashi; ③ Kashi aims to triple the 5,000 RMB (about US$ 738.55) duty-free quota that Hainan province was authorized to implement as an offshore duty-free policy in 2010, so that tourists will be exempted from paying tax on items totaling up to 15,000 RMB (about US$ 2215.66) per visit.

Kashi, with its 2,000-year history, has an obligation to balance its development as an economic zone with the preservation of its heritage. Environmentally-friendly development with a low carbon emission, sustainable development strategy has been confirmed as the future direction for this oasis city with its fragile environment.

"Shenzhen has been the star city in the first 30 years since the reform and opening policy was adopted; Kashi will be the star city in the next 30 years." This is the expectation of all the people of Kashi. In 2013, President Xi Jinping proposed the Belt and Road Initiative. One of the goals of the Initiative is to boost economic growth in Xinjiang. Xinjiang, once the heart of the ancient Silk Road, is prepared to play a central role in the Belt and Road Initiative. With the restoration to its former importance, Kashi will be a key stop on the Silk Road of the 21st century. (665 words)

Difficult Sentences

① Meanwhile, the southern coastal city of Shenzhen, the pioneer city in the reform and opening and the country's original Special Economic Zone, entered into a cooperation agreement with Kashi.

与此同时，南方沿海城市深圳与喀什签订了合作协议。深圳是中国改革开放的窗口，也是国家创建的首个经济特区。

② On November 18, 2011, the Kashi government announced the "5th-generation new city" initiative. The core component of a 5th-generation city's development is reliance on the service economy, chiefly about finance, tourism and logistics, boosted by the values of low consumption and high output.

2011年11月18日，喀什市政府宣布将喀什打造成为"第五代新型城市"。在低能耗和高产出理念的推动下，第五代新型城市的发展核心是金融、旅游和物流等服务性产业。

③ ... Kashi aims to triple the 5,000 RMB (about US$ 738.55) duty-free quota that Hainan province was authorized to implement as an offshore duty-free policy in 2010, so that tourists will be exempted from paying tax on items totaling up to 15,000 RMB (about US$ 2215.66) per visit.

从2010年起，海南省执行"离岛免税"政策，免税额度为5000元人民币(约为738.55美元)。喀什市政府计划将免税额度定为其3倍，也就是说，喀什一次性旅游购物的免税额度将达到15,000元人民币(约为2215.66美元)。

Text 2 China Is Pushing Ahead in New Fronts of Science and Technology Development

China used to be a world leader in science and technology in history, however, since the 14th century, it has gradually lagged behind the world. After the founding of the People's Republic of China, the country has made great progress in science and technology. Recently, it is pushing ahead in new fronts of science and technology development. From wind power to nuclear reactors to high-speed rail, it is already outpacing U.S. efforts and moving aggressively to capture the lead.

I. High-speed Rail

China's high-speed railway network had a total track length of 37,900 km by the end of 2020, ranking top in the world. The new high-speed railways not only shorten travel time, but also feature high technology and an environmentally friendly design. Fuxing bullet trains, China's domestically developed and manufactured bullet trains, can travel at speeds of up to 350 kilometers per hour. They also make less noise and consume less energy. On January 2017, Fuxing bullet trains were put into commercial operation on the Beijing-Shanghai high-speed railway. On December 30 that same year the CR400 BF-C intelligent Fuxing bullet train set achieves automatic driving speed of 350 km/h on the Beijing-Zhangjiakou high-speed railway. On June 25, 2021, Fuxing bullet trains were operated in the Tibet autonomous region, signifying that all provincial-level regions in mainland China had access to high-speed train services. The high-speed lines demonstrate China's strong capability to build high-tech and green high-speed railway and infrastructure.

II. Alternative Energy

China has striven to develop alternative energy including wind power and biomass energy in recent years as the world's largest energy market continues to shift away from dirty coal power toward cleaner fuels. China is installing wind power at a faster rate than any other nation in the world, and manufactures 40 percent of the world's solar photovoltaic (PV) systems. ① It is home to three of the world's top ten wind turbine manufacturers and five of the top ten silicon-based PV manufacturers in the world. China is the first country in the world to extract flammable ice using a horizontal well-drilling technique. Natural gas hydrate is commonly known as flammable ice. In 2017, China announced to have extracted a record amount of flammable ice and industrialized gas hydrate extraction.

III. Supercomputing

Supercomputing affects the possibility to do cutting-edge scientific research in many areas, including nuclear energy, nanotech and materials science, and other advanced biotech applications. In December, 2020, Chinese scientists have created the world's first photonic quantum computer prototype, called Jiuzhang, which can solve a problem no classical supercomputer can tackle within a reasonable amount of time. ② Jiuzhang, named after an ancient Chinese mathematical text[1], can perform an extremely sophisticated calculation, called Gaussian boson sampling[2] in 200 seconds. The same task would take the world's fastest classical supercomputer, Fugaku, around 600 million years.

IV. Medical Technology and Biotechnology

③ In 1965, the Biochemistry Institute synthesized crystalline bovine insulin, a bioactive protein. China thus became a world leader in this research field. ④ BGI (Beijing Genomics Institute) has been described as having the world's largest DNA sequencing facilities. ⑤ China aims and has made progress towards becoming a world leader in regenerative medicine which also includes areas such as tissue engineering and gene therapy. Biotechnology will be used to enhance economic development as well as for improving Chinese environmental protection, nutrition, healthcare, and medicine. In 2015, the Nobel Prize for Physiology or Medicine was awarded to Tu Youyou whose research led to the discovery of artemisinin, a crucial new treatment for malaria. The discovery of artemisinin and its use in treating malaria are regarded as a significant breakthrough in tropical medicine in the 20th century. It is also a major health improvement for people in developing tropical countries in south Asia, Africa, and South America.

V. Satellite Launching Technology

China successfully developed and launched scientific experimental satellites, retrievable satellites and stationary communication satellites, ⑥ mastering the advanced techniques of satellite retrieval and multiple satellites launching with a single carrier rocket and synchro-positioning technology. Tianwen 1, the country's first independent Mars mission, was launched by a Long March 5 heavy-lift carrier rocket in 2020. Tianwen 1 landed its rover on the red planet on May 15, 2021. In the coming days, the rover, which was recently named Zhurong after an ancient Chinese god of fire, is scheduled to observe and map the landing site and then leave the capsule to roam the landing area for scientific surveys.

In November, 2020, China launched the Chang'e 5 probe as part of its moon missions. After sampling lunar soil, Chang'e 5's reentry capsule set off for Earth and landed, marking the accomplishment of China's first return with samples from an extraterrestrial celestial body. China is expected to build an international lunar research station

---

1 中国量子计算机原型之所以取名为"九章",是为了纪念中国古代张苍、耿寿昌所撰写的一部数学专著《九章算术》。该书内容十分丰富,总结了战国、秦、汉时期的数学成就。它的出现标志中国古代数学形成了完整的体系,是一部具有里程碑意义的历史著作。

2 高斯玻色取样的本质就是生成模拟信号,是蒙特卡洛模拟。在数字计算机中实现的蒙特卡洛模拟,是通过软件来实现的模拟,而玻色取样则是通过硬件来实现的蒙特卡洛模拟。

on the moon's south pole in the future.

In 2020, China successfully launched the 55th satellite of the BeiDou Navigation Satellite System by using a Long March 3B rocket, marking the completion of the deployment of its own global navigation system. Beidou is China's largest space-based system and one of four global navigation networks. The system began to provide basic global services in 2018.

Other achievements in high technology are represented by the successful explosion of atomic and hydrogen bombs, the launching of the Long March series carrier rocket and the research in satellite telecommunications and superconductivity. In all these fields, China has either reached or approached advanced world levels. (917 words)

Difficult Sentences

① It is home to three of the world's top ten wind turbine manufacturers and five of the top ten silicon-based PV manufacturers in the world.
中国已有三家公司跻身于世界风力涡轮机制造商十强的行列，全球十大硅基光伏生产商中有五家是中国公司。

② Jiuzhang, named after an ancient Chinese mathematical text, can perform an extremely sophisticated calculation, called Gaussian boson sampling in 200 seconds.
"九章"以中国古代数学专著《九章算术》命名，它可以在200秒内处理"高斯玻色取样"这样复杂的计算。

③ In 1965, the Biochemistry Institute synthesized crystalline bovine insulin, a bioactive protein.
1965年，中国科学院生物化学研究所人工合成了具有生物活性的蛋白质-结晶牛胰岛素。

④ BGI (Beijing Genomics Institute) has been described as having the world's largest DNA sequencing facilities.
中国科学院北京基因组研究所拥有世界上最大的DNA序列测定实验室。

⑤ China aims and has made progress towards becoming a world leader in regenerative medicine which also includes areas such as tissue engineering and gene therapy.
中国致力于成为包括组织工程和基因治疗等领域在内的再生医学领域的世界领导者，并已取得了一定的进展。

⑥ ...mastering the advanced techniques of satellite retrieval and multiple satellites launching with a single carrier rocket and synchro-positioning technology.
中国还掌握了卫星回收、一箭多星和同步定位的先进技术。

Unit 5 Economy, Science and Technology

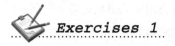 **Exercises 1**

Task 1 Short Answer Questions

Directions: *Read Text 1 and Text 2 and then answer the following questions briefly.*

1. Compared with Shenzhen, what's the disadvantage of Kashi?
2. What's the main industry in Kashi?
3. Which provincial-level region is the last to get high-speed train service in China?
4. Why is the rover named Zhurong?
5. How much money can tourists spend in Kashi bonded area without paying tax?

Task 2 Reading Comprehension

Part A

Directions: *Complete the following five sentences with the proper forms of the words given in the brackets.*

1. Language develops with the _____ (emerge) and development of society.
2. In 1980, the first inland _____ (economy) development zone was built in Shenzhen.
3. In the past 50 years, China has _____ (succeed) developed and launched many man-made satellites.
4. To protect our fragile environment, industrialized countries should reduce their energy _____ (consume) as much as possible.
5. The creation of an efficient and _____ (sustain) transport system is critical to the long-term future of Beijing.

Part B

Directions: *In this section, you are going to read a passage with 5 statements attached to it. Each statement contains information given in one of the paragraphs. Identify the paragraph from which the information is derived. Each paragraph is marked with a letter.*

A) Kashi, located in the southwestern part of Xinjiang Uygur Autonomous Region, has a history of more than 2,000 years. It has occupied an important position in northwestern China since ancient times. Situated at the juncture of the southern and northern routes of the Old Silk Road, it attracted merchants from many parts of the world to trade here. So Kashi became a famous trading city, called a bright pearl on the Old Silk Road.

B) Meanwhile, Kashi is also a national historical and cultural city. Etigar Mosque, the largest mosque in Xinjiang, situated on Etigar Square in the center of the city, is more than 500 years old. The city has produced many famous figures throughout its history.

C) Kashi is divided into two parts: the new district and the old district. In the new district, the streets are wide and lined with high-rise buildings, little different from other cities in China; in the old district, many narrow streets still have "bazaar" as part of their names. From the names of these streets people can imagine the past glory of this ancient city on the Old Silk Road. Local government aims to rebuild the old district and retains its original appearance.

D) State Council has approved the general plans for building a 50-square-kilometer economic zone in Kashi. The central and local governments have injected 1.82 billion yuan ($297 million) into the massive project to upgrade the basic infrastructure. 15 transport arteries have already been completed.

E) Other construction projects concerning infrastructure—including water, electricity and auxiliary roads—are expected to be finished in 2013. Gas pipelines will be in place next year.

F) The preferential policies, including tax exemptions, subsidized electricity and transportation rates, low-interest loans for infrastructure projects and construction of better rail and air links with neighboring countries will bring prosperity and stability to this age-old city.

( ) 1. Kashi is an important historical and cultural city with the largest mosque in Xinjiang located here.

( ) 2. It is hoped that preferential policies adopted by the economic zone will bring prosperity to Kashi.

( ) 3. In ancient times, Kashi was a flourishing trading city, a bright pearl on the Old Silk Road.

( ) 4. Uygur ethnic group can use electricity, gas pipeline in the near future.

( ) 5. Walking along the streets, tourists can not only admire the modern buildings but also imagine the past glory of this ancient city.

Task 3 Translation

Directions: *Translate the following passage from Chinese into English.*

喀什，意为"玉石之国"，是古丝绸之路上举足轻重的城市。她不仅是中国向西方探索、寻求开放的贸易通道，也是多民族融合交汇的走廊。喀什是一座以维吾尔族为主要居民的古老城市，民族特色浓郁，80%的人口是维吾尔族同胞，信奉伊斯兰教，因此整个城市风貌、商业、礼仪、娱乐、宗教活动都围绕着他们固有的方式展开。

Task 4 Writing

Directions: *After reading Text 1, we have a general idea of the Kashi and its prospect. You are required to carry out a research on the first Special Economic Zone in China—Shenzhen and find out the similarities and differences between Kashi and Shenzhen from the perspective of their patterns of economic development.*

Unit 5 *Economy, Science and Technology*

Section B Listening and Speaking

> **Text 3** Situational Dialogue: China's Manned Submersible[1]

(A: a Chinese student, Li Dong;   B: his classmate, Tony—an exchange student)

A: Hi, Tony. What are you busy doing?

B: ① I'm reading a Chinese book named *Pilgrimage to the West*.

A: This is one of the Four Chinese Classical Novels. Do you like it?

B: ② Yes, I am very interested in the chapter that Monkey King dived into the deep sea and obtained a magic weapon from the Dragon King of the Eastern Sea. Then he began to make himself master of the four quarters.

A: This is also my favorite part. In my teens, I wished I could dive to the deep sea as Money King did.

B: It's impossible to dive to the sea floor as Monkey King did.

A: No, a Chinese manned submersible Jiaolong carrying three people has successfully reached to the depth of 7,062 meters into the Mariana Trench[2] in the Pacific Ocean in 2012. In 2020, the deep-sea manned submersible Fendouzhe set a new national diving record of 10,909 meters in the Mariana Trench.

B: Oh, it's really a piece of exciting news. But why do people call it Jiaolong? What a strange name for a submersible!

A: According to Chinese legend, the Dragon King lived in a palace on the sea floor. So the Jiaolong is named after the mythical sea dragon.

B: What did the scientists do under the deep-sea water?

A: It's reported that the Jiaolong got three water samples and made several scientific experiments on the sea floor. Fendouzhe carrying three experts conducted scientific research for about six hours on the bed of the Mariana Trench.

B: Is China the only country who can carry out deep-sea exploration?

---

1 China's Manned Submersible：中国载人潜水器。
2 马里亚纳海沟是目前（截至2012年）所知最深的海沟，也是地壳最薄之处，形成据估计已有6000万年。该海沟处在亚洲大陆和澳大利亚之间。全长2,550千米，为弧形，平均宽70千米，大部分水深在8,000米以上。最深处为11,034米，是地球的最深点。

A: No. I knew that the U.S., Russia, France, Japan all have carried out the deep-sea exploration, but China has achieved a leading position in the world in the field of manned deep diving.

B: Congratulations! By the way, in what aspect can the submersible be used?

A: ③ It can be used in many aspects, such as oceanography, underwater archaeology, ocean exploration, etc.

B: It seems you know a lot about the submersible. Could you give me a brief introduction of it?

A: With pleasure. A submersible is a small vehicle designed to operate underwater. It relies on a support facility or vessel for replenishment of power and breathing gases.

B: Are all the submersibles manned?

A: ④ No, there are two types of submersibles, including both manned and unmanned craft, otherwise known as remotely operated vehicles or ROVs. China's unmanned submersible Haidou-1 has set a new record by submerging 10,907 meters under the Pacific Ocean's surface at the Mariana Trench in 2020.

B: It must have cost Chinese government much money to carry out deep-sea exploration.

A: Yes. China has invested 470 million yuan (73.79 million US dollars) into the Jiaolong project for submersible research and modification and on-sea experiment.

B: I remember your major is ocean engineering Maybe someday you can be a member of them.

A: I hope so.

B: Hope you can realize your dream. (517 words)

 Difficult Sentences

① I'm reading a book named *Pilgrimage to the West*.

我正在读《西游记》。(《西游记》是中国四大名著之一，另一英文翻译法为 *Journey to the West*。)

② I am very interested in the chapter that Monkey King dived into the deep sea and obtained a magic weapon from the Dragon King of the Eastern Sea. Then he began to make himself master of the four quarters.

《西游记》中，我喜欢孙悟空潜入海底，从东海龙王那里获得宝物金箍棒，从此开始称霸四方的那一章。

③ It can be used in many aspects, such as oceanography, underwater archaeology, ocean exploration, etc.

许多方面都会用到潜水器，例如海洋研究、水下考古以及大洋考察等等。

④ No, there are many types of submersibles, including both manned and unmanned craft, otherwise known as remotely operated vehicles or ROVs.

目前，深海探测技术领域主要包括载人和无人两种潜水器，后者也被称为遥控潜水器或者ROV。

Unit 5 Economy, Science and Technology

Text 4 A Tour Guide Commentary on Qinghai-Tibet Railway

Hello, passengers. Welcome to take our train from Qinghai to Tibet. During the journey, we will run through a range of mountains, a world of lakes, herds of endangered animals, and encounter many diverse ethnic groups. Now, I will give you a general introduction of it.

The Qinghai-Tibet Railway, with many world records, is the world's highest railroad which is 4,000 meters above sea level and the world's longest plateau railway stretching from the ancient city of Xining in Qinghai province to Lhasa, Tibet autonomous region. It has a total length of 1,956 kilometers, with about 550 kilometers of the tracks running on frozen earth. The maximum speed of the Tibet Train can reach 120 km/h in common area, and 100 km/h in the frozen soil area. The average altitude along the Tibet railway is 4,600 meters with temperature droping to –30°C. It is more a monument of human construction than a railway.

There are 45 stations along the Qinghai-Tibet Railway with Tanggula railway station, at 5,068 meters, being the world's highest railway station. As everybody knows, permafrost is a big challenge for engineers. In summer, the uppermost layer thaws, and the ground becomes muddy. ① Engineers dealt with this problem by building elevated tracks with foundations sunk deep into the ground, building hollow concrete pipes beneath the tracks to keep the rail bed frozen, and using metal sun shades. Due to their efforts, we can enjoy such a magnificent view of the plateau.

Along the Qinghai-Tibet railway, nine scenery viewing platforms have been set up. You can find fertile plains of the Yangtze, the Yellow and Lantsang Rivers; the Qaidam Basin, one of China's largest basins; Qaidam's Qarham Lake, Asia's largest salt lake, over which the world's longest salt lake bridge was erected; ② the Kunlun Mountains, hailed as "the origin of ten thousand mountains," a prominent pilgrimage site for Buddhists from around the world; the Geladaintong glaciers[1] near the snow-covered Tanggula Mountain range; ③ the vast bleakness of Hoh Xil[2] Nature Reserve and northern Tibet's Young Tun Basin, a paradise for rare wildlife such as the Tibetan antelope, wild yak and Tibetan wild donkey.

Qinghai-Tibet Railway was the region's first rail link with the outside world. As the first extension line of the Qinghai-Tibet Railway, the Lhasa-Shigatse Railway was operational in 2014.

Qinghai-Tibet Railway

---

1 格拉丹东冰川位于格尔木市唐古拉山乡境内。藏语意为"高高尖尖的山峰",海拔6620米,是青海、西藏两省区天然分界线,也是青藏线109国道的最高点。有南北两条呈半弧形的大冰川。格拉丹东冰川地段是青藏铁路全线气候条件最恶劣、地质条件最差、施工难度最大的区段。
2 可可西里国家级自然保护区:"可可西里"蒙语意为"青色的山梁",位于青藏高原西北部,夹在唐古拉山和昆仑山之间,是长江的主要源区之一。可可西里自然保护区是目前世界上原始生态环境保存最完整的地区之一。

Fuxing bullet trains, powered by both internal-combustion and electricity with a designed speed of 160 km per hour, was put into use on the Lhasa-Nyingchi Railway starting in June, 2021. Tibet is opening her arms to welcome the tourists home and abroad.

That's my introduction of the Qinghai-Tibet railway. I hope you enjoy the view and the journey. Thank you. (452 words)

 Difficult Sentences

① Engineers dealt with this problem by building elevated tracks with foundations sunk deep into the ground, building hollow concrete pipes beneath the tracks to keep the rail bed frozen, and using metal sun shades.

专家们采取了以桥代路、通风管路基、保温板等方法终于攻克了冻土上架设铁路的难题。

② ...the Kunlun Mountains, hailed as "the origin of ten thousand mountains," a prominent pilgrimage site for Buddhists from around the world...

昆仑山脉被喻为"万山之宗",是全世界佛教信徒朝拜的圣地

③ ...the vast bleakness of Hoh Xil Nature Reserve and northern Tibet's Young Tun Basin, a paradise for rare wildlife such as the Tibetan antelope, wild yak and Tibetan wild donkey.

面积广阔的可可西里自然保护区以及西藏北部的羌塘盆地是野生动物藏羚羊、牦牛、野驴的天堂。

 Exercises 2

Task 1 Listening Comprehension

Directions: *Listen to the Situational Dialogue in Text 3, read the four choices marked A, B, C and D, and decide which is the best answer.*

1. Which of the following books is mentioned in the dialogue?
   A. *A Dream of Red mansions.*   B. *Pilgrimage to the West.*
   C. *Romance of Three Kingdoms.*   D. *Water Margin.*

2. In 2020, how many meters has the deep-sea manned submersible Fendouzhe dived in the Mariana Trench?
   A. 10,909.   B. 7062.   C. 10,907.   D. 10,709.

3. What did the Chinese scientists do under the deep-sea water?
   A. Collect core samples.   B. Take water samples
   C. Measure the seawater temperature   D. Take sea floor pictures

4. In which field has the manned submersible not been used?
   A. Oceanography.   B. Underwater archaeology.

C. Ocean engineering. D. Ocean exploration.

5. How does a submersible replenish its power and breathing gases?

   A. It has self-replenishment capacity.

   B. It is still a mystery to the public.

   C. It needn't to be replenished for many days.

   D. It depends on a support facility or vessel.

Task 2 Spot Dictation

Directions: *You will hear the passage based on Text 4 three times. When the passage is read for the first time, you should listen carefully for its general idea. When the passage is read for the second time, you are required to fill in the blanks with the exact words you have just heard. Finally, when the passage is read for the third time, you should check what you have written.*

The Qinghai-Tibet Railway, stretching from the ancient city of Xining in Qinghai province to Lhasa, Tibet autonomous region is the world's highest railroad and the world's longest plateau railway. Its total length is 1,956 kilometers, among which about 550 kilometers of the tracks is running on frozen earth. The Tibet Train goes at the (1)_____ speed of the 120 km/h in common area and 100 km/h in the frozen soil area. It is more a (2)_____ of human construction than a railway.

As everybody knows, permafrost is a big (3)_____ for engineers. In the summer, the uppermost layer thaws, and the ground becomes muddy. Engineers (4)_____ this problem by building elevated tracks with foundations sunk deep into the ground, building hollow concrete pipes beneath the tracks to keep the rail bed frozen. Because of their efforts, we can enjoy such a (5)_____ view of the plateau.

Along the Qinghai-Tibet railway, nine scenery viewing platforms have been (6)_____. You can find fertile plains of rivers and the world's longest salt lake bridge (7)_____ over Qaidam's Qarham Lake—Asia's largest salt lake. The Kunlun Mountains, hailed as "the origin of ten thousand mountains" is a (8)_____ pilgrimage site for Buddhists from around the world. The vast bleakness of Hoh Xil Nature (9)_____ and northern Tibet's Young Tun Basin is a paradise for rare wildlife such as the Tibetan antelope, wild yak and Tibetan wild donkey.

When you take the train, you will run through a range of mountains, a world of lakes, herds of endangered animals, and (10) encounter many diverse _____. It will be fascinating journey.

Task 3 Short Answer Questions

Directions: *After reading Text 3 and Text 4, answer the following questions briefly.*

1. What is the Jiaolong named after?

2. What's the other name for the unmanned submersible?

3. How much did the Chinese government spend on Jiaolong project?

4. What's the average altitude of the Qinghai-Tibet railway?

5. What kind of rare wild animals can be found in Hoh Xil Nature Reserve and Young Tun Basin?

Task 4 Translation

青藏铁路是世界上最高的铁路，在海拔超过4000米的青藏高原上运行，从青海西宁到西藏拉萨，全长1956公里，其中550公里穿过永久冻土带。青藏铁路沿途设有45座车站，唐古拉车站，堪称世界上海拔最高的车站。修建青藏铁路最大的挑战是永久冻土。夏天气温上升，最上面冻土融化，路就塌了；冬天温度降低，冻土膨胀，把建在上面的钢轨顶起来。这个难题最终被聪明能干的中国工程人员解决了。

Words and Expressions for Economy, Science and Technology

Text 1	
dwindle	v. 衰败，衰退
renaissance	n. 复兴
Special Economic Zone	经济特区
ecological environment	生态环境
innovation	n. 改革
logistics	n. 物流
recruit	v. 招收，补充
infrastructure	n. 基础设施
explicit	adj. 清楚的，直白的
boom	n. 繁荣
bonded area	保税区
duty-free quota	免税额度
Belt and Road Initiative	"一带一路"倡议
Text 2	
"Sea Wing" underwater glider	"海鹰"水下滑翔机
saline soil	盐碱土
photovoltaic	adj. 光电的
cutting-edge	adj. 最前沿的
nanotech	n. 纳米技术
wind turbine	风力涡轮机
materials science	材料科学
flammable ice	可燃冰
natural gas hydrate	天然气水合物
photonic quantum computer prototype	量子计算机原型

Gaussian boson sampling	高斯玻色取样
supercomputer Fugaku	日本"富岳"超级计算机
biotech	*adj.* 生物技术的
China's National University of Defense Technology	国防科技大学
artemisinin	*n.* 青蒿素
malaria	*n.* 疟疾
carrier rocket	运载火箭
atomic and hydrogen bombs	原子弹和氢弹
Zhurong Rover	火星探测车"祝融"号
extraterrestrial celestial body	地外天体
lunar research station	月球科研站
BeiDou Navigation Satellite System	北斗导航系统
Text 3	
submersible	*n.* 潜水器
Pilgrimage to the West	《西游记》
Mariana Trench	马里亚纳海沟
oceanography	*n.* 海洋学，海洋研究
replenish	*v.* 补给，补充
ocean engineering	船舶工程
Text 4	
Tanggula	唐古拉
permafrost	*n.* 永久冻土
Lantsang River	澜沧江
Qaidam Basin	柴达木盆地
Qaidam's Qarham Lake	察尔汗盐湖
endangered animals	濒危动物
frozen earth	冻土
thaw	*v.* 融化
Lhasa-Shigatse	拉萨–日喀则
Lhasa-Nyingchi	拉萨–林芝
hail	*v.* 誉为

Key to Exercises

Before You Start

1. Kashi, located at the western edge of Xinjiang Uygur autonomous region has an area of 162,000 square kilometers and a population of approximately 3.5 million. It features a desert climate with hot summers and cold winters. Kashi was the last Chinese town along the Silk Route where the northern and southern arms of the Silk Road converged on their way to the Mediterranean. In order to boost the economy in Kashi region, the government classified the area as a Special Economic Zone, the sixth one in China, in May 2010. Kashi is facing a bright future.
2. China has made great progress in science and technology since 1949. In some fields China has achieved or approached advanced world levels, for example: Five-hundred-meter Aperture Spherical Radio Telescope (FAST), C919 large airliner, quantum computer, trial for rice production in saline soil, launch of Chinese-built aircraft carrier, "Sea Wing" underwater glider, first extraction of combustible ice, operations of Phase IV of Shanghai Yangshan Automated Deep Water Port, the cross-sea bridge linking Hong Kong, Zhuhai and Macao, and running of Fuxing bullet trains, manned and unmanned submersible.

 Exercises 1

Task 1 Short Answer Questions

1. Kashi has a fragile ecological environment and comparatively poorer neighborhood.
2. Kashi mainly depends on service economy, including finance, tourism, logistics.
3. Tibet autonomous region.
4. The rover was named Zhurong after an ancient Chinese god of fire.
5. It can amount to 15,000 RMB or US$2215.

Task 2 Reading Comprehension
Part A

1. emergence   2. economic   3. successfully   4. consumption   5. sustainable

Part B

1. B   2. F   3. A   4. E   5. C

Task 3 Translation

Kashi which means "the country of jade" is the city of significance along the Old Silk Road. It not only symbolizes China's effort to explore the West for trade but also represents the hub of multi-ethnic minorities' interactions. Kashi is an old city where the Uygur ethnic minority has constituted the bulk of its population. They account for 80 percent and hold the belief of Islamism. Consequently the entire city evolves around this unique feature in a range of activities, including city construction, commerce, etiquette, entertainment as well as religious ceremonies.

Task 4 Writing
Sample Writing

The Similarity and Difference between Kashi and Shenzhen

Shenzhen and Kashi have something in common. Both of them are the windows on the opening policy in China. As Special Economic Zones in China, they both get great support from the Chinese government in investment and policy preference.

However, they are different in several aspects. In the first place, they are situated in different zones. Shenzhen is a coastal city facing countries in Southeast Asia, so it has great opportunities to obtain foreign investment. While, as an inland city, what Kashi faces are those comparatively poorer neighboring regions, therefore it has little advantage in this respect.

In the second place, Kashi can make full use of its geographical advantage to develop service economy, chiefly about finance, logistics. Shenzhen developed its economy by the quick expansion of industries and building up of a significant population. Kashi's fragile ecological environment prohibits it from doing so. Environmentally-friendly development with a low carbon emission, sustainable development strategy is the future direction of Kashi's development.

Moreover, as the important city in Silk Road, Kashi has special character in his history and culture. Kashi's Old City is called "the best-preserved example of a traditional Islamic city to be found anywhere in Central Asia", where eastern culture and western culture converge. The priority should be given to tourism industry rather than manufacturing industry as Shenzhen does.

Shenzhen has been the star city in the past 30 years; Kashi will be the star city in the next 30 years. (250 words)

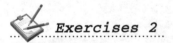

Exercises 2

Task 1 Listening Comprehension
1. B   2. A   3. B   4. C   5. D

Task 2 Spot Dictation
1. maximum   2. monument   3. challenge   4. dealt with
5. magnificent 6. set up   7. erected   8. prominent
9. Reserve   10. ethnic groups

Task 3 Short Answer Questions
1. The dragon king lived in the sea.
2. ROV(remotely operated underwater vehicles)
3. 470 million yuan or 73.79 million US dollars.
4. 4600 meters above the sea level.
5. Tibetan antelopes, wild yaks and Tibetan wild donkeys.

Task 4 Translation
The Qinghai-Tibet Railway is supposed to be the highest railway in the world, stretching from Xining, Qinghai province to Lhasa, Tibet, crossing the more-than-4,000 meters Tibetan Plateau along the way. It covers a distance of 1,956 kilometers, 550 kilometers of which is the permanent frozen earth (permafrost). It contains altogether 45 stations, one of which, Tanggula Station, boasts to be the highest station in the world. The formidable obstacle in the construction of the railway is permafrost. In the summer when the temperature rises, the surface will melt and collapse. In the winter when the temperature drops, the permafrost will expand, causing the bumping of railway road. Finally, the obstacle has been solved by the capable Chinese engineers.

Unit

Chinese Holidays and Folk Customs

导 读

本单元着重介绍中国春节、端午节、七夕等传统节日的来历和习俗，包括节日的起源演变、典故传说、传统与现代的庆祝方式等，旨在通过对中国传统节日和民俗的介绍，使学生能够运用所学中国文化知识及相关的英语表达进行跨文化交流，弘扬中华节日文化。

Before You Start

While you are preparing for this unit, think about the following questions:

1. How many Chinese traditional holidays can you list out? Which holidays are you most familiar with? Could you introduce one of them in detail in the light of its origin, history and features, and describe how people celebrate it?
2. Discuss how people in the past celebrated some other Chinese traditional holidays and how modern people celebrate these holidays in different ways.

Section A Reading and Writing

Text 1 Chinese New Year in the Modern World: A Traditional Chinese Holiday Today

Chinese New Year (also called the Spring Festival) is celebrated each year by millions of people throughout the world and viewed as the most significant traditional Chinese holiday. ① The 15-day holiday celebration encompasses many traditional feasts, decorations, and symbolism relating to the history of the holiday and the desire for good luck in the new year.

Symbolism

② Each year in the Chinese calendar is identified by one of the 12 animals in Chinese astrology: rat, ox, tiger, rabbit,

dragon, snake, horse, sheep, monkey, rooster, dog and pig. These animal zodiacs all have great significance in Chinese astrology and are celebrated during Chinese New Year.

History

Like many Chinese holidays, the origins of Chinese New Year celebrations are rooted in legend. According to an ancient story, a village was being tormented by a monster called "Nian", which looked like either a dragon or a unicorn, with a horn on the head and an extremely large mouth, capable of swallowing several people in a single bite. Nian lived deep at the bottom of the sea all year round and climbed up the shore only on New Year's Eve to devour the cattle and kill people's lives. The villagers tried to keep the monster from eating their families by setting out large portions of food. Later, they discovered Nian was afraid of loud noises, as well as of the color red. Then, whenever Nian would appear, they would hang red lanterns and light fireworks. This would scare the monster away.

Time Frame

Chinese New Year lasts for 15 days, starting with the Lunar New year's Day and ending with the Lantern Festival on the night of the fifteenth day. Each day of Chinese New Year has its own significance and set of festivities that are to take place. For instance, on New Year's Eve, many Chinese gather with family for an elaborate reunion dinner where they discuss the past year and catch up. It is essential entertainment for the Chinese to sit together to make and eat jiaozi and simultaneously watch the New Year's Gala held by CCTV. The first day of the new year is for visiting and honoring elderly family members and welcoming various Chinese gods; the second day is set aside for prayer to ancestors and for married daughters to visit their parents. Other days of the Chinese New Year are for staying at home, going to the market, having reunion dinners, or visiting and dining with relatives or friends. People will greet one another by saying "Xinnian kuaile/hao," which literally means "Happy New Year," or "Gongxi facai," meaning "Congratulations and Prosperity."

Features

A traditional aspect of Chinese New Year is the giving of red envelopes or packets with money as gifts to younger friends and relatives, and the gifting of these packets is thought to bring luck to the receivers in the new year.

Fireworks and firecrackers are also used during the Chinese New Year. The noise of the fireworks is thought to be so loud that any evil spirits nearby will be scared away, bringing luck and prosperity to those that celebrate the holiday.

Ensuring good fortune in the coming year is a big part of the Chinese New Year. People prepare for New Year's Eve by cleaning out their houses and decorating them with things considered to be lucky. ③ Certain flowers and fruits, posters or statues of lucky gods and the color red are considered auspicious, such as red Spring Couplets, paper-cuts, "upside-down Fu," and door gods.

Influence

In modern China, Chinese New Year creates the world's largest mass movement of people as many workers in Chinese communities are given up to a week off work. Unmarried young people and married men with their wives and children are expected to pay a visit to their parents and grandparents. With the modern world dividing family and spreading them out, the Chinese New Year holiday becomes more important to Chinese people than ever before. Although the holiday is known for its noisy fireworks, mass movement of travelers and elaborate parties, it remains a special day in the hearts of Chinese people for its emphasis on family. (707 words)

Difficult Sentences

① The 15-day holiday celebration encompasses many traditional feasts, decorations, and symbolism relating to the history of the holiday and the desire for good luck in the New Year.
持续15天的春节庆典活动包括传统美食家宴，富有节日特色和寓意的装饰与象征，以及人们对新一年的美好期盼。

② Each year in the Chinese calendar is identified by one of the 12 animals in Chinese astrology...
中国农历的每一年都被冠之以一种动物的名称，中国占星术中一共有12种动物……

③ Certain flowers and fruits, posters or statues of lucky gods and the color red are considered auspicious, such as red Spring Couplets, paper-cuts, "upside-down Fu," and door gods.
某些花果，代表喜庆的各路神仙的年画或雕像，以及红色的东西，如春联、剪纸、倒福字、门神等，都具有吉祥的寓意。

Text 2 The Dragon Boat Festival

Falling on the 5th day of the 5th month according to the Chinese lunar calendar, the Dragon Boat Festival (also called Duanwu Festival) is of great significance. It has been held annually for more than 2,000 years and is notable for its educational influence. Many legends circulate around the festival but the most popular is the legend of Qu Yuan. This festival is celebrated to commemorate the patriotic poet Qu Yuan (340 BC—278 BC), and also acts as a chance for Chinese people to build their bodies and dispel diseases.

Qu Yuan was a minister of the State of Chu and one of China's earliest poets. ① In face of great pressure from the powerful Qin State, he advocated enriching the country and strengthening its military forces so as to fight against Qin. However, he was opposed by aristocrats headed by Zi Lan, and later deposed and exiled by King Huai. In his exiled days, he still cared much for his country and people and composed immortal

poems including Li Sao (The Lament), Tian Wen (Heavenly Questions) and Jiu Ge (Nine Songs), which had far-reaching influences. ② In 278 BC, he heard the news that Qin troops had finally conquered Chu's capital, so he finished his last masterpiece Huai Sha (Embracing Sand) and plunged himself into the Miluo River, clasping his arms to a large stone.

On hearing of Qu Yuan's death, all the local people nearby were in great distress. The fishermen sailed their boats up and down the river to look for his body. People threw into the water zongzi (pyramid-shaped glutinous rice dumplings wrapped in reed or bamboo leaves) and eggs to divert possible fish or shrimps from attacking his body. ③ An old doctor poured a jug of realgar wine (Chinese liquor seasoned with realgar) into the water, hoping to turn all aquatic beasts drunk.

Because Qu Yuan died on the fifth day of the fifth lunar month, people decided to commemorate him on that day every year. Dragon boat racing and eating zongzi have become the central customs of the festival. Dragon boats are thus named because the fore and stern of the boat is in a shape of traditional Chinese dragon. A team of people works the oars in a bid to reach the destination before the other teams. One team member sits at the front of the boat beating a drum in order to maintain morale and ensure that the rowers keep in time with one another. The races are held among different clans, villages and organizations, and the winners are awarded medals, banners, jugs of wine or festive meals. When making the special food zongzi, soaking the glutinous rice, washing the reed or bamboo leaves and wrapping zongzi with leaves are the most important parts. Today, this custom prevails in China and other countries. For two thousand years,

传统粽型香囊

Qu Yuan's patriotic spirit has influenced numerous people and he remains revered by the people from all over the world.

On the Dragon Boat Festival, parents may dress their children up with a perfume pouch. ④ They first sew little bags with colorful silk cloth, then fill the bags with perfumes or herbal medicines, and finally string them with silk threads. The perfume pouch will be hung around the neck or tied to the front of a garment as an ornament. It is said to be able to ward off evil. (571 words)

Difficult Sentences

① In face of great pressure from the powerful Qin State, he advocated enriching the country and strengthening its military forces so as to fight against Qin.
面对强大秦国的逼迫,他力主富国强兵,奋起抗秦。

② In 278 BC, he heard the news that Qin troops had finally conquered Chu's capital, so he finished his last masterpiece "Huai Sha" (Embracing Sand) and plunged himself into the Miluo River, clasping his arms to a large stone.

公元前278年，屈原在得知秦军攻破楚国国都后，奋笔疾书写下了绝世名作《怀沙》，之后抱石投汨罗江而死。

③ An old doctor poured a jug of realgar wine (Chinese liquor seasoned with realgar) into the water, hoping to turn all aquatic beasts drunk.

一位老郎中还把一壶雄黄酒倒入江中，希望能药晕蛟龙水兽。

④ They first sew little bags with colorful silk cloth, then fill the bags with perfumes or herbal medicines, and finally string them with silk threads.

他们先用彩绸缝制成一个个小袋子，在里面装上香料或中草药，然后用丝线串成一串。

Exercises 1

Task 1 Short Answer Questions

Directions: *Read Text 1 and Text 2 and then answer the following questions briefly.*

1. Why did villagers hang red lanterns and set off fireworks during Chinese New Year, according to the legend?
2. Normally when does Chinese New Year start and end?
3. What activities will most Chinese families hold on Chinese New Year's Eve?
4. How did Qu Yuan die?
5. What are the most popular customs of the Dragon Boat Festival?

Task 2 Reading Comprehension

Part A

Directions: *In this section, there are 5 incomplete sentences. You are required to select one word for each blank from a list of choices given in the word bank below. You may not use any of the words in the bank more than once.*

| essential | spread out | set aside | emphasis | prosperity |
| prevail | be rooted in | oppose | fortune | notable for |

1. Charlotte Brontë is _____ several good novels, among which her masterpiece is *Jane Eyre*.
2. The central government may put more _____ on spurring economic growth.
3. It's easier to swim with the tide than to _____ the views of the majority.
4. There can be no durable development and _____ without peace.
5. You need to _____ some time every week to work on your relationships, your health, recreation and your spiritual self.

Part B

Directions: *In this section, you are going to read a passage with five statements attached to it. Each statement contains information given in one of the paragraphs. Identify the paragraph from which the information is derived. Each paragraph is marked with a letter.*

A) The Dragon Boat Festival has a history of more than 2,000 years and is notable for its educational influence. Many legends circulate around the festival but the most popular is the legend of Qu Yuan. This festival is celebrated to commemorate the patriotic poet Qu Yuan (340 BC—278 BC), and also acts as a chance for Chinese people to build their bodies and dispel diseases.

B) Qu Yuan was an official in the State of Chu. His talent aroused envy and hatred of his partner, an aristocrat named Zi Lan, who managed to have Qu Yuan dismissed and expelled out of the capital. In the year of 278 BC, Chu had been conquered by another empire, Qin. Grief-stricken, Qu plunged into the river by clinging himself to a stone and ended his life. On hearing of Qu Yuan's death, all the local people nearby were in great distress. People threw into the water zongzi and eggs to divert possible fish or shrimps from attacking his body.

C) Because Qu Yuan died on the fifth day of the fifth lunar month, people decided to commemorate him on that day every year. Dragon boat racing and eating zongzi have become the central customs of the festival. Dragon boats are thus named because the fore and stern of the boat is in a shape of traditional Chinese dragon. When making the special food zongzi, soaking the glutinous rice, washing the reed or bamboo leaves and wrapping zongzi with leaves are the most important parts. Today, this custom prevails in China and other countries. For two thousand years, Qu Yuan's patriotic spirit has influenced numerous people and he remains revered by the people from all over the world.

D) On Dragon Boat Festival, parents may dress their children up with a perfume pouch. The perfume pouch will be hung around the neck or tied to the front of a garment as an ornament. It is said to be able to ward off evil.

( ) 1. Perfume pouches worn by kids on the Dragon Boat Festival are said to have the function of getting rid of evil.

( ) 2. Qu Yuan's loyalty to his country has been deeply appreciated by people both in the past and in modern world.

( ) 3. Famous for its educational function and its role of reminding people of staying healthy, the Dragon Boat Festival has been celebrated for a long time.

( ) 4. Local people were very sad at Qu Yuan's death.

( ) 5. Zongzi was poured into the river to prevent the fish and shrimps from biting Qu Yuan's body.

Task 3 Translation

Directions: *Translate the following passage from Chinese into English.*

中国新年，又称春节，是中国最重要的传统节日。春节的庆祝活动从除夕开始一直延续到元宵节，即从农历腊月的最后一天至正月的第十五天。各地欢度春节的习俗和传统有很大差异，但通常每个家庭都会在除夕夜团聚，一起吃年夜饭。为驱厄运、迎好运，家家户户都会进行大扫除。人们还会在门上粘贴红色的对联（couplets），对联的主题为健康、发财和好运。其他的活动还有放鞭炮、发红包和探亲访友等。

Task 4 Writing

Direction: *Nowadays, western festivals such as Christmas and Valentine's Day are gaining increasing popularity in China, especially among college students. Think about this phenomenon and write an article entitled* **Should Young People Celebrate Western Festivals instead of Chinese Traditional Festivals**? *Your writing should be based on the outline given in Chinese below.*

1. 很多年轻人喜欢过西方节日而忽视了中国传统节日；
2. 一些中老年人对此颇有微词；
3. 我的看法。

Section B Listening and Speaking

Text 3 Situational Dialogue: Our Traditional Holidays—Still Meaningful?

(*On the day after Christmas*)

Liu Yan: A great holiday just passed, what happened to you? How many mysterious gifts and sweet words have you received?

Xiao Qi: Come on! It's just a western festival.

Li Bin: Yeah. We have so many traditional festivals that have been ignored. Now it is popular for young people to celebrate western festivals. What's the reason?

Wang Li: The day before yesterday I received a lot of presents from my boyfriend. ① Personally I think the best aspect of western festivals is that people can send each other some significant small gifts and improve their relationship.

Xiao Qi: I can only partly agree with you. Sending gifts is also frequently seen in Chinese holidays, especially in the Spring Festival.

Li Bin: ② True, our festivals can stimulate the consumption more than western festivals. But that's just why I think some traditional festivals have lost their meanings. People waste too much money on buying food, decorations and presents.

Liu Yan: I agree. Moreover, people eat and drink too much, which is harmful to their health. And many usually can't really relax themselves in the holidays.

Xiao Qi: Yeah. For example, in the Spring Festival, we should have a good rest during the vacation. On the contrary, we are all busy visiting or entertaining others. ③ We have to maintain a series of social relationships, thus engaged in various social activities.

Wang Li: I remember my childhood during the Chinese New Year. I was very busy, but I was not engaged in buying gifts. I involved myself in preparing for the coming programs, especially for New Year's Eve. We made food and decorations ourselves. ④ On the first day of the Chinese New Year, there would be a variety of performances all over the country, such as stilt walking, Yangko dancing and dragon or lion dancing. Unfortunately, many of such activities have disappeared. Now we often either watch TV or play mahjong or PC games at home!

Li Bin: I think our holiday is too tiresome and lacking in romance. Christmas in the west is mysterious and romantic for Chinese. Santa Claus is so lovely. Valentine's Day is more romantic; I hope that every day is Valentine's Day.

Xiao Qi: You can desire, but your boyfriend never craves it.

Liu Yan: Actually we also have romantic festivals; I believe that the Double Seventh Festival in China is more romantic than Valentine's Day. We also have stories with deep impression, which may be heart-warming and impressive. If the lovers regard the day as the most important festival it will be more significant. And then we can say goodbye to Western Valentine's Day.

Wang Li: ⑤ Yeah, we need to treasure our traditional holidays, but we should not exclude all the western festivals, right?

Xiao Qi: Definitely. The west festivals will help us to understand western culture. If the foreigners also celebrate our traditional holidays, that can be called the exchange of the culture. (502 words)

stilt walking

dragon dancing

Difficult Sentences

① Personally I think the best aspect of western festivals is that people can send each other some significant small gifts and improve their relationship.

我觉得西方节日最好的一面是可以让人们互赠一些有意义的小礼物，增进感情。

② True, our festivals can stimulate the consumption more than western festivals.

没错，我们的节日比西方节日更能刺激消费。

③ We have to maintain a series of social relationships, thus engaged in various social activities.

我们不得不去维系各种社会关系，参加各类社交应酬。

④ On the first day of the Chinese New Year, there would be a variety of performances all over the country, such as stilt walking, Yanko dancing and dragon or lion dancing.
每到大年初一，全国上下都会有各种表演，像踩高跷、扭秧歌、舞龙舞狮等。

⑤ Yeah, we need to treasure our traditional holidays, but we should not exclude all the Western holidays, right?
是的，我们必须珍惜我们的传统节日，但也不能完全排斥西方节日。

Text 4 A Speech on Double Seventh Festival

Good morning, ladies and gentlemen,

Today I'm very glad to stand here to make a speech about a Chinese Valentine's Day. Do you know what it is? Yes, it's called the Double Seventh Festival, on the 7th day of the 7th lunar month, a traditional festival full of romance. It often goes into August in the Gregorian calendar.

This festival is in mid-summer when the weather is warm and the grass and trees reveal their luxurious greens. At night when the sky is dotted with stars, and people can see the Milky Way spanning from the north to the south. On each bank of it is a bright star, which sees each other from afar. ① They are the Cowherd and the Weaver Maid, and about them there is a beautiful love story passed down from generation to generation.

Long, long ago, there was an honest and kind-hearted fellow named Niu Lang (the Cowherd). His parents died when he was a child. Later he was driven out of his home by his sister-in-law. So he lived by himself herding cattle and farming. One day, a fairy from heaven called Zhi Nü (the Weaver Maid) fell in love with him and came down secretly to earth and married him. The Cowherd farmed in the field and the Weaver Maid wove at home. They lived a happy life and gave birth to a boy and a girl. Unfortunately, the God of Heaven soon found out the fact and ordered the Queen Mother of the Western Heavens to bring the Weaver Maid back. With the help of celestial cattle, the Cowherd flew to heaven with his son and daughter. ② At the time when he was about to catch up with his wife, the Queen Mother took off one of her gold hairpins and made a stroke. One rushing river appeared in front of the Cowherd. The Cowherd and the Weaver Maid were separated on the two banks forever and could only feel their tears. ③ Their loyalty to love touched magpies, so tens of thousands of magpies came to build a bridge for the Cowherd and the Weaver Maid to meet each other. The Queen Mother was eventually moved and allowed them to meet each year on the 7th of the 7th lunar month. Hence their meeting date has been called "Qixi" (Double Seventh).

④ Today some traditional customs are still observed in rural areas of China, but have been weakened or diluted in urban cities. However, the legend of The Cowherd and the Weaver Maid has taken root in the hearts of the people. In recent years, in particular, urban youths have celebrated "Qixi" as Valentine's Day in China. As a result, owners of flower shops, bars and stores are full of joy as they sell more commodities for love. (475 words)

 Difficult Sentences

① They are the Cowherd and the Weaver Maid, and about them there is a beautiful love story passed down from generation to generation.

他们是牛郎星和织女星,关于他们的美丽爱情故事代代相传。

② At the time when he was about to catch up with his wife, the Queen Mother took off one of her gold hairpins and made a stroke.

在他马上就要追上妻子的时候,王母娘娘取下一根金钗,用力一划。

③ Their loyalty to love touched magpies, so tens of thousands of magpies came to build a bridge for the Cowherd and the Weaver Maid to meet each other.

他们对爱情的坚贞感动了鹊鸟,成千上万只鹊鸟赶来架起了一座鹊桥,让牛郎织女得以相会。

④ Today some traditional customs are still observed in rural areas of China, but have been weakened or diluted in urban cities.

如今在中国的乡村人们仍然保持了一些传统习俗,但在城市这些习俗却不被重视,已经渐渐淡化了。

 Exercises 2

Task 1 Listening Comprehension

Directions: *Listen to the Situational Dialogue in Text 3, read the four choices marked A, B, C and D, and decide which is the best answer.*

1. When does the conversation happen?
   A. Before a western holiday.   B. After a western holiday.
   C. Before a Chinese holiday.   D. After a Chinese holiday.
2. What's the greatest significance of western festivals?
   A. Receiving mysterious gifts and sweet words.
   B. Exchanging small presents and promoting further understanding.
   C. Stimulating the consumption in the domestic market.
   D. Making diverse decorations for the houses and apartments.

Unit 6 *Chinese Holidays and Folk Customs*

3. What's the main reason for many Chinese festivals' having lost their meanings?

   A. They are very boring. B. The are energy-consuming.

   C. They are money-consuming. D. They are lacking in romance.

4. Which of the following activities was not included during the Chinese New Year many years ago?

   A. Yangko dancing. B. Dragon dancing.

   C. Stilt walking. D. Mooncake making.

5. In what way does Wang Li advise young people to celebrate domestic and foreign festivals?

   A. We could celebrate Chinese traditional holidays as well as western festivals.

   B. We should eliminate western festivals while keeping Chinese traditional holidays.

   C. We should celebrate Chinese traditional holidays instead of western ones.

   D. We should celebrate western festivals and foreigners need to celebrate Chinese holidays.

Task 2 Spot Dictation

Directions: *In this section you will hear a passage taken from Text 4 **three times**. When the passage is read for the first time, you should listen carefully for its general idea. When the passage is read for the second time, you are required to fill in the blanks with the exact words you have just heard. Finally, when the passage is read for the third time, you should check what you have written.*

Long, long ago, there was an honest and kind-hearted fellow named Niu Lang (the Cowherd). His parents died when he was a child. Later he was (1)_____ out of his home by his sister-in-law. So he lived by himself herding (2)_____ and farming. One day, a fairy from heaven called Zhi Nü (the Weaver Maid) fell in love with him and came down (3)_____ to earth and married him. The Cowherd farmed in the field and the Weaver Maid wove at home. They lived a happy life and (4)_____ a boy and a girl. Unfortunately, the God of Heaven soon found out the fact and ordered the Queen Mother of the Western Heavens to bring the Weaver Maid back. With the help of celestial cattle, the Cowherd (5)_____ with his son and daughter. At the time when he was about to (6)_____ his wife, the Queen Mother took off one of her gold hairpins and made a stroke. One rushing river appeared in front of the Cowherd. The Cowherd and the Weaver Maid were (7)_____ on the two banks forever and could only feel their tears. Their (8)_____ to love touched magpies, so tens of thousands of magpies came to build a bridge for the Cowherd and the Weaver Maid to meet each other. The Queen Mother was (9)_____ moved and allowed them to meet each year on the 7th of the 7th lunar month. (10)_____ their meeting date has been called "Qi Xi" (Double Seventh).

Task 3 Short Answer Questions

Directions: *Read Text 4 and answer in brief the following questions.*

1. What's the weather like around the Double Seventh Festival?

2. How did Niu Lang make a living after he was driven out by his sister-in-law?
3. Who helped Niu Lang to fly to heaven?
4. Who built a bridge for Niu Lang and Zhi Nü to meet each year?
5. Do people in modern cities celebrate the Double Seventh Festival?

Task 4 Translation

Directions: *Translate the following passage from Chinese into English.*

中国的许多传统节日，包括七夕在内，都是在农业社会的基础上形成的。随着时代的推移，社会形势发生了很大的变化，原先孕育这些节日的环境也起了变化，因此人们也不像以前那样重视这些节日了。例如，提起七夕节，现在的年轻人想到的大多是"鲜花""巧克力""烛光晚餐"等，这些通常都是西方情人节的特征。近年来，节假日已然变成了消费日，商场搞起了形式多样的促销，打出各种各样的广告。

Words and Expressions for Talking about China

Text 1	
the Spring Festival	春节
encompass	*v.* 包括
animal zodiac	动物生肖
catch up	叙旧
fireworks and firecrackers	烟花爆竹
the Lantern Festival	元宵节
New Year's Gala	春晚
red envelope or packet	红包
Spring Couplet	春联
paper-cut	*n.* 剪纸
upside-down Fu	倒"福"字
door god	门神
New Year's Eve	除夕
torment	*n. & v.* 折磨
unicorn	*n.* 独角兽
auspicious	*adj.* 吉祥的
Text 2	
lunar calendar	农历
commemorate	*v.* 纪念
aristocrat	*n.* 贵族
dispel diseases	祛除疾病
advocate	*v.* 倡导
compose	*v.* 作（词、诗等）

depose	v. 废黜
exile	v. 流放
masterpiece	n. 名作
award medals	授予奖章
prevail	v. 流行
numerous people	广大人民
patriotic spirit	爱国精神
revere	v. 尊崇，尊敬
herbal medicine	草药
ornament	n. 装饰物
realgar	n. 雄黄
aquatic	adj. 水生的
glutinous rice	糯米
perfume pouch	香囊
Text 3	
stimulate the consumption	刺激消费
eat and drink too much	暴饮暴食
stilt walking	踩高跷
Yanko dancing	扭秧歌
dragon or lion dancing	舞龙舞狮
play mahjong	打麻将
tiresome	adj. 无聊的
be lacking in romance	缺乏浪漫
heart-warming	adj. 感人的，暖心的
exclude	v. 排斥，排除
Text 4	
Gregorian calendar	阳历
mid-summer	n. 仲夏
Milky Way	银河
be dotted with stars	缀满星星
pass down from generation to generation	代代相传
the Cowherd	牛郎
the Weaver Maid	织女
herd cattle	牧羊
fairy	n. 仙子；小精灵
celestial	adj. 天上的，天空的

续表

hairpin	*n.* 发簪
magpie	*n.* 喜鹊
rushing river	汹涌的大河
dilute	*v.* （使）稀释；削弱，降低
loyalty to love	对爱情的坚贞

Unit 6 *Chinese Holidays and Folk Customs*

Key to Exercises

Before You Start

1. Chinese New Year(the Spring Festival), the Lantern Festival, Qingming Festival (Tomb Sweeping Festival, Tomb Sweeping Day, Clear and Bright Festival), the Dragon Boat Festival, the Mid-Autumn Festival, the Double Seventh Festival(Qixi), the Double Ninth Festival, etc.

Sample introduction of the Lantern Festival:

The Lantern Festival falls on the 15th day of the first month of the lunar new year. Because the first lunar month is called yuan-month and in the ancient times people called night "Xiao". The 15th day is the first night to see a full moon. So the day is also called Yuan Xiao Festival in China.

According to the Chinese tradition, at the very beginning of a new year, when there is a bright full moon hanging in the sky, there should be thousands of colorful lanterns hung out for people to appreciate. At this time, people will try to solve the puzzles on the lanterns and eat yuanxiao (glutinous rice ball) and get all their families united in the joyful atmosphere.

History

Until the Sui Dynasty in the sixth century, Emperor Yangdi invited envoys from other countries to China to see the colorful lighted lanterns and enjoy the gala(节日的，庆祝的) performances.

At the beginning of the Tang Dynasty in the seventh century, the lantern displays would last three days. The emperor also lifted the curfew(宵禁令), allowing the people to enjoy the festive lanterns day and night. In the Song Dynasty, the festival was celebrated for five days and the activities began to spread to many of the big cities in China. Colorful glass and even jade were used to make lanterns, with figures from folk tales painted on the lanterns.

Origin

There are many different beliefs about the origin of the Lantern Festival. But one thing for sure is that it had something to do with religious worship.

One legend tells us that it was a time to worship Taiyi, the God of Heaven in ancient times. The belief was that the God of Heaven controlled the destiny of the human world. He had sixteen dragons at his beck and call and he decided when to inflict drought, storms, famine or pestilence(瘟疫) upon human beings. Beginning with Qinshihuang, the first emperor to unite the country, all subsequent emperors ordered splendid ceremonies each year. The emperor would ask Taiyi to bring favorable weather and good health to him and his people. Emperor Wudi of the Han Dynasty directed special attention to this event. In 104 BC, he proclaimed it one of the most important celebrations and the ceremony would last throughout the night.

2. About celebrating the Spring Festival:

Many customs accompany the Spring Festival. Some are still followed today, while others have weakened.

Customs in the past:

1. Preparations began several days before the Spring Festival. The 23rd day of the 12th lunar month was called Preliminary Eve. At this time, people offered sacrifice to the kitchen god. After the Preliminary Eve, people began preparing for the coming New Year. This is called "Seeing the New Year in." Store owners were busy then as everybody went out to purchase necessities for the New Year. Materials not only included edible oil, rice, flour, chicken, duck, fish and meat, but also fruits, candies and all kinds of nuts. What's more, various decorations, new clothes and shoes for the children as well as gifts for the elderly, friends and relatives, were all on the list of purchasing;

2. Sweeping the dust. "Sweeping the dust" before the Spring Festival means a thorough cleaning of houses to sweep away bad luck in the past year. This custom shows a good wish of putting away old things to welcome a new life;

3. Pasting Spring Couplets, paper-cuts and "upside-down Fu";

4. Staying up late on New Year's Eve;

5. Pasting New Year prints. The most famous ones are Door Gods, Surplus Year after Year, Three Gods of Blessing, Salary and Longevity, An Abundant Harvest of Crops, Thriving Domestic Animals and Celebrating Spring.

6. Temple Fair. The temple fair is a place for people to appreciate the traditional arts and entertainments.

7. People in northern China would eat jiaozi, or dumplings, for breakfast, as they thought "jiaozi" in sound meant "bidding farewell to the old and ushering in the new". Southern Chinese ate niangao (New Year cake made of glutinous rice flour) on this occasion.

8. Dragon or lion dances with drummers once were extremely popular in the Chinese New Year celebration.

Popular customs in modern times:

1. Decorating the house with the color red, like red Spring Couplets, paper-cuts and "upside-down Fu."

2. Holding reunions and having great feasts on New Year's Eve.

3. Watching the New Year's Gala on New Year's Eve and other distinctive entertaining TV Games during the Festival.

4. Visiting relatives and friends, sending gifts to each other and giving red envelopes to kids.

5. People send New Year wishes to each other via mobile phone short messages, Wechat or telephone calls.

6. Setting off the fireworks and firecrackers.

7. Working people normally have seven days off work to celebrate the Spring Festival.

8. Some urban dwellers choose to travel to their hometown or abroad, while quite a lot farmers like playing mahjong at home.

Unit 6 *Chinese Holidays and Folk Customs*

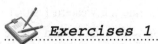 **Exercises 1**

Task 1 Short Answer Questions

1. Because they discovered the monster Nian was afraid of loud noises and the color red.

2. It starts with the Lunar New year's Day and ends with the Lantern Festival on the night of the fifteenth day.

3. They hold a family reunion, having dinner together, making and eating jiaozi and watching the New Year's Gala.

4. He plunged himself into the Miluo River, clasping his arms to a large stone.

5. Dragon boat racing and eating zongzi.

Task 2 Reading Comprehension
Part A
1. notable for   2. emphasis   3. oppose   4. prosperity   5. set aside

Part B
1—D   2—C   3—A   4—B   5—B

Task 3 Translation

Chinese New Year, also called the Spring Festival, is the most important traditional Chinese holiday. New Year celebrations run from Chinese New Year's Eve, the last day of the last month of the lunar calendar, to the Lantern Festival on the 15th day of the first month. Customs and traditions concerning the celebration of the Chinese New Year vary widely from place to place. However, New Year's Eve is usually an occasion for Chinese families to gather for the annual reunion dinner. It is also customary for every family to thoroughly clean the house in order to sweep away ill fortune and to bring in good luck. And doors will be decorated with red couplets with themes of health, wealth and good luck. Other activities include lighting firecrackers, giving money in red envelopes, and visiting relatives and friends.

Task 4 Writing
Sample Writing

Should Young People Celebrate Western Festivals Instead of Chinese Traditional Festivals?

Nowadays western festivals have enjoyed great popularity among Chinese young people such as Christmas and Valentine's Day. And some young people simultaneously ignore our Chinese traditional holidays. Opinions differ about this phenomenon.

While young people regard celebrating western festivals as a fashion, old people in China make some complaints. They condemn that young people have forgotten our precious traditions and customs which fully convey the beauty and essence of Chinese culture and the spirit of Chinese people.

Personally, I don't think it sensible for our young people to celebrate the western festivals while giving up the Chinese traditional festivals. First of all, Chinese traditional festivals have been the particular icons of Chinese culture, which are the most precious cultural heritage that we have inherited from our ancestors. As a new generation in China, we should shoulder the responsibility of protecting and spreading them so that our offspring can enjoy and learn them in the long future. Secondly, the traditional festivals offer good opportunities for family reunion and the expansion of social interactions. Without work and study tasks, people go back home and hold family parties, fully enjoying the happy family life thanks to the traditional festivals.

To sum up, I firmly believe that young people should cherish our traditional festivals. Moreover, they can also celebrate the western festivals for fun and for the sake of cross-cultural communication. (238 words)

Exercises 2

Task 1 Listening Comprehension

1. B 2. B 3. C 4. D 5. A

Task 2 Spot Dictation

1. driven   2. cattle   3. secretly   4. gave birth to   5. flew to heaven
6. catch up with   7. separated   8. loyalty   9. eventually   10. Hence

Task 3 Short Answer Questions

1. The weather is warm and the grass and trees reveal their luxurious greens.
2. He made a living by herding cattle and farming.
3. Celestial cattle.
4. Magpies.
5. Yes, especially urban youths. They celebrate it as Valentine's Day in China.

Task 4 Translation

Many traditional Chinese festivals, including the Double Seventh Festival, develop on the setting of agricultural society. With the passage of time, social situations have altered greatly and so has the setting from which these festivals arise. As a result, people no longer value these festivals as before. For example, speaking of the Double Seventh Festival, young people mostly associate it with flowers, chocolate and candlelight dinner, which usually characterize Valentine's Day in the west. In recent years, the festivals have shifted into consumption days in that various promotional activities and advertisements are launched in department stores.

Unit 7

Land of Splendor

导 读

　　本单元旨在通过对中国山河的自然美景和文化意蕴进行介绍，帮助学生掌握相关的语言表达，使他们能够在跨文化交际中流畅地向外国友人介绍中国的美景，弘扬中华文化。

Before You Start

While you are preparing for this unit, think about the following questions:

1. Many scenic places in China are inseparable from Chinese philosophies. Would you please introduce one of the places to us and describe its natural beauty and cultural connotation in detail?
2. Confucius said, "The wise enjoy the waters; the benevolent enjoy the mountains." What's your understanding of the saying?

Section A　Reading and Writing

Text 1　The Yellow River

　　The Yellow River or *Huanghe*, the second longest river in China at 5,464 kilometers, wanders through seven provinces and two autonomous regions in north China. ① As the Chinese regard yellow as an emblem of the loess land, the emperor, the yellow skin and the legendary Chinese Dragon, therefore the Chinese refer to the river as not just a river, but "the Mother River" and "the Cradle of the Chinese Civilization."

　　30,000 years ago, the ancient Chinese started to live by the shore of the Yellow River and played the overture of the ancient Chinese civilization. The ashes which date back to 10,000 years ago spread all over the Yellow River basin. It is the birthplace of the ancient

Chinese civilization and was the most prosperous region in early Chinese history. 6,000 years ago, as a representative of the matriarchal culture, Banpo clan existed on the loess land of north China.

The Yellow River's top attractions include forest parks, deserts, grasslands, the Hukou Waterfall, the Loess Plateau, and ancient cities. Along the Yellow River, one can not only fully enjoy the natural scenery, but also explore the Chinese history and culture.

Upper Reaches Attractions—Mountains, Valleys, and Grasslands

♦ **Qinghai—the Source**

The Yellow River (along with the Yangtze and the Mekong) begins in Yushu Tibetan Prefecture of Qinghai province. This is an inhospitable, high-altitude, mountain country, but the Qinghai-Tibet Railway runs through it. You can see the land of the upper reaches of China's greatest rivers and much more on a Xi'an-Lhasa Express Tour.

♦ **Gansu—Upper Bridging Point**

② Lanzhou is the first major city on the Yellow River and has long had the only bridge over the Yellow River in the region, making it a key stop on the Silk Road. Lanzhou has many attractions centered around the Yellow River, like the Zhongshan Iron Bridge, the Waterwheel Garden, and the Five Springs Mountain.

♦ **Ningxia—Forests, Deserts, and Grasslands**

The river water here is clear and flows steadily. The Yellow River benefits the people living on both sides irrigating the farmland to make it fertile.

Yinchuan, nicknamed the Phoenix City, is the capital of Ningxia Hui autonomous region. Located on the Yellow River, it was once the capital of the Western Xia Empire and historically served as a trade route town becoming prosperous because of its convenient location between western Chinese cities such as Urumqi and the eastern ones such as Beijing and Shenyang.

Zhongwei in west Ningxia offers Shapotou, one of the most beautiful deserts in China, with the Yellow River flowing through, and Tonghu Grassland, an "Eden within the Desert."

♦ **Inner Mongolia—Pristine Grasslands**

In Inner Mongolia, the Tomb of Genghis Khan and the Singing Sands of Ordos are definitely must-sees, where tourists can experience Mongolian nomadic pastoral life on the Ordos Grasslands.

Middle Reaches Attractions—The Loess Plateau

♦ **Shaanxi/Shanxi—Land of Yellow Soil and Chinese Origins**

The Hukou Waterfall ("Teapot Mouth" Waterfall), 400km (250 miles) from Xi'an, is the most spectacular waterfall on the Yellow River, where the yellow waters are funneled and poured like tea from a giant teapot.

③ The Hukou Waterfall is near Yan'an, the historic Communist headquarters at the end of the Long March, where Mao Zedong, Zhou Enlai and others, living in loess dugouts, devised strategies to fight against the Japanese invaders. Yan'an also has the Mausoleum of the Yellow Emperor, China's legendary ancestor.

Pingyao Ancient Town in Shanxi province is the closest tourist destination to the Hukou Waterfall, with lots of ancient architecture.

♦ Luoyang—Ancient Capital and Buddhist Holy Land

Luoyang is one of the eight ancient capitals in China. It is called the city of peony, which has over 1500 years' history in planting. Luoyang is the city with the most complete varieties and the best flower nature. In April every year, the blossoming of peony overflows the city and decorates Luoyang like paradise. The Longmen Grottoes are some of the most famous Buddhist grottoes in China.

Lower Reaches Attractions—The Northern Plain

♦ Zhengzhou—Ancient Capital and Kung Fu Birthplace

Zhengzhou is one of the eight ancient capitals of China. Zhengzhou Yellow River Scenic Area is a typical large Chinese recreational park 30km NW of Zhengzhou, offering temples, historic statues, hills to ramble up, and views of the Yellow River. About two-hours' drive away from Zhengzhou is the world-famous Shaolin Temple, the birthplace of Shaolin Kung Fu, where the cultural and natural scenery is breathtaking.

♦ Kaifeng—Ancient Capital with a Jewish Quarter

Kaifeng, another of China's eight ancient capitals, has many ancient architectural attractions, including the Iron Pagoda, the Pota Pagoda, Shanxi-Shaanxi-Gansu Guild Hall, and the Remains of Mosque of Judaism. (788 words)

 Difficult Sentences

① As Chinese regard yellow as an emblem of the loess land, the emperor, the yellow skin and the legendary Chinese Dragon, therefore Chinese refer to the river as not just a river, but "the Mother River" and "the Cradle of the Chinese Civilization."

在中国人眼中，黄色是黄土地的颜色，是皇帝的象征，是肌肤的颜色，是中国龙的象征，因此，黄河不仅仅是一条河，更是"母亲河"，是"中华文明的摇篮"。

② Lanzhou is the first major city on the Yellow River and has long had the only bridge over the Yellow River in the region, making it a key stop on the Silk Road.
兰州是黄河流域的首个大城市，也是长久以来该地区唯一的跨河大桥所在地，因此兰州成为丝绸之路上的重镇。

③ The Hukou Waterfall is near Yan'an, the historic Communist headquarters at the end of the Long March, where Mao Zedong, Zhou Enlai and others, living in loess dugouts, devised strategies to fight against the Japanese invaders.
壶口瀑布距离延安不远。长征结束后延安是中共中央所在地。毛泽东、周恩来以及其他领导人在黄土高坡的窑洞里运筹帷幄，取得了抗战的胜利。

Text 2 The Great Wall

The Great Wall, like the Pyramids of Egypt, the Taj Mahal in India and the Hanging Garden of Babylon, is one of the great wonders of the world.

① The Great Wall was continuously built from the 7th century BC to the 17th century AD on the northern border of the country as the great military defense project of successive Chinese Empires, with a total length of more than 20,000 kilometers, thus known as the Ten Thousand Li Wall in China. It begins in the east at Shanhaiguan Pass in Hebei Province and ends at Jiayuguan Pass in Gansu Province to the west.

Historical records trace the construction of the origin of the Wall to defensive fortification back to the year 656 BC during the reign of King Cheng of the State of Chu. Its construction continued throughout the Warring States Period in the fifth Century BC when ducal states Yan, Zhao, Wei, and Qin were frequently plundered by the nomadic peoples living north of the Yinshan and Yanshan mountain ranges. Walls, then, were built separately by these ducal states to ward off such harassments. Later in 221 BC, when Qin conquered the other states and unified China, Emperor Qinshihuang ordered the connection of these individual walls and further extensions to form a united defense system against invasions from the north.

A separate outer wall was constructed north of the Yinshan range in the succeeding Han Dynasty (202 BC—220 AD), which went to ruin through years of neglect. In the many intervening centuries, succeeding dynasties rebuilt parts of the Wall. The most extensive reinforcements and renovations were carried out in the Ming Dynasty (1368 AD—1644 AD) when altogether 18 lengthy stretches were reinforced with bricks and rocks, hence the Great Wall becoming the world's largest military structure. It is mostly the Ming Dynasty Wall that visitors see today.

The Great Wall is divided into two sections, the east and the west, with Shanxi Province as the dividing line. The west part is a rammed earth construction, about 5.3 meters high on average. In the eastern part, the core of the Wall is rammed earth as well, but the outer shell is reinforced with bricks and rocks. The most imposing and best preserved sections of the Great Wall are at Badaling and Mutianyu, on the outskirts of Beijing and both are open to visitors.

The Wall of those sections is 7.8 meters high and 6.5 meters wide at its base, narrowing to 5.8 meters on the ramparts, wide enough for five horses to gallop abreast. There are ramparts, embrasures, peep-holes and apertures for archers on the top, besides gutters with gargoyles to drain rain-water off the parapet wall. Two-storied watch-towers are built at approximately 400-meters intervals.

The top stories of the watch-towers were designed for observing enemy movements, while the first stories were used for storing grain, fodder, military equipment and gunpowder as well as for quartering garrison soldiers. The highest watch-tower at Badaling standing on a hill-top, is reached only after a steep climb, like "climbing a ladder to heaven." The view from the top is rewarding, however. ② The Wall follows the contour of mountains that rise one behind the other until they finally fade and merge with distant haze.

A signal system formerly existed that served to communicate military information to the dynastic capital. This consisted of beacon towers on the Wall itself and on mountain tops within sight of the Wall. At the approach of enemy troops, smoke signals gave the alarm from the beacon towers in the daytime and bonfire did this at night. Emergency signals could be relayed to the capital from distant places within a few hours long before the invention of anything like modern communications.

There stand 14 major passes (Guan "关", in Chinese) at places of strategic importance along the Great Wall, the most important being Shanhaiguan and Jiayuguan. Yet the most impressive one is Juyongguan, about 50 kilometers northwest of Beijing.

The Great Wall reflects collision and exchanges between agricultural civilizations and nomadic civilizations in ancient China. ③ It provides significant physical evidence of the far-sighted political strategic thinking and mighty military and national defense forces in ancient China, and is an outstanding example of the superb military architecture, technology and art of ancient China. It embodies unparalleled significance as the national symbol for safeguarding the security of the country and its people. Its historic and strategic importance is matched only by its architectural significance. (751 words)

 Difficult Sentences

① The Great Wall was continuously built from the 7th century BC to the 17th century AD on the northern border of the country as the great military defense project of successive Chinese Empires, with a total length of more than 20,000 kilometers, thus known as the Ten Thousand Li Wall in China.

长城是公元前7世纪至公元17世纪中国历代君主下令在北部疆界修建的伟大军事防御工程。它全长两万多千米，在中国被称为"万里长城"。

② The Wall follows the contour of mountains that rise one behind the other until they finally fade and merge with distant haze.

长城依着山势蜿蜒起伏,直至消失在远方的雾霭中。

③ It provides significant physical evidence of the far-sighted political strategic thinking and mighty military and national defense forces in ancient China, and is an outstanding example of the superb military architecture, technology and art of ancient China.

长城为古代中国远见卓识的政治战略思想和强大的军事国防力量提供了重要的实物证据,堪称中国古代军事建筑、技术和艺术的杰出典范。

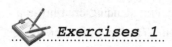

Exercises 1

Task 1 Short Answer Questions

Directions: *Read Text 1 and Text 2 first and then answer the following questions briefly.*

1. Historically, what contributed to the economic success of Yinchuan?
2. What is Yan'an famous for?
3. How many provinces/autonomous regions does the Yellow River run through?
4. Why was the Great Wall constructed?
5. How did the garrison soldiers on the Great Wall communicate military information?

Task 2 Reading Comprehension

Directions: *In this section, there is a passage with ten blanks. You are required to select one word for each blank from the word bank above the passage. You may not use any of the words in the bank for more than once.*

| anthem | preserved | construction | collision | consolidation |
| hardships | legacy | renovations | unparalleled | ward |

The Great Wall is (1) _____ in the world in its scale and span of construction, as well as for the great quantities of labor and the degree of difficulties involved.

The (2) _____ of the Great Wall started in the 7th century BC and completed in the 17th century AD, lasting for more than 2000 years. It has undergone three major (3) _____ in the Qin, Han, and Ming dynasties. The Great Wall of today is mainly the (4) _____ of the Ming-Dynasty renovations. It meanders for 20,000 kilometers on top of the mountains. The 600-kilometer-long section in the northern outskirts of Beijing is the best (5) _____.

The Great Wall played a significant role in history. It served as a military defense project to (6) _____ off harassments from the nomadic peoples living north of the Yinshan and Yanshan mountain ranges. The Great Wall reflects (7) _____ and exchanges between agricultural civilizations and nomadic civilizations in ancient China.

The (8) _____ involved in building the Great Wall are beyond imagination. Numerous people had to leave their homes and families to go north, where they toiled for years. Many lost their lives on the worksites.

Over the centuries, the Great Wall has become a symbol of (9) _____ and strength for the Chinese people. It symbolizes that great achievement can be made with a common will and concerted effort. The national (10) _____ , composed during the War of Resistance Against Japanese Aggression (1931—1945), calls on the people to "amount our flesh and blood towards our new Great Wall!"

Task 3 Translation

Directions: Translate the following passage from Chinese into English.

黄河，全长5464千米，仅次于长江，是中国第二长的河流。黄河发源于青藏高原的青海省。它向东流经7个省和两个自治区，最后注入渤海。黄河被称为"中华民族的母亲河"，也被誉为"中华文明的摇篮"，因为黄河流域是古代中华文明的发祥地。黄河流域也是中国古代历史上最繁荣和人口最密集的地区。宋元以前，该地区一直是中国经济发展的重心，创造了当时世界上最发达的文明。

Task 4 Writing

Directions: By 2022, China has 56 World Heritage properties, with 14 of them being Natural Heritage and four being both Natural and Cultural Heritage. Please carry out a survey on what the Chinese people have done in preserving the precious natural and cultural heritage properties of the world.

Section B   Listening and Speaking

Text 3 Situational Dialogue: The Summer Palace

(A: Tour guide; B: Tourist)

A: Welcome to the Summer Palace! It is up to now the best preserved and the largest imperial garden in China with the richest landscapes and concentrated buildings. It is renowned as one of the four famous gardens in China.

B: I've been to the Chengde Summer Resort, which is said to be one of the gardens too. What are the other two?

A: The Humble Administrator's Garden and the Lingering Garden, both in Suzhou, Jiangsu province. They are fantastic.

B: Oh, look at the scenery here, splendid! And the architecture, breathtakingly beautiful!

A: That's it! The Summer Palace is a monument to classical Chinese architecture, in terms of both garden design and construction. ① Borrowing scenes from surrounding landscapes, it radiates not only the grandeur of an imperial garden but also the beauty of nature in a seamless combination that best illustrates the guiding principle of traditional

Chinese garden design: "The works of men should match the works of Heaven."

B: Look at this building! It kind of resembles the Hall of Supreme Harmony in the Forbidden City. What's it called?

A: This is the Hall of Benevolence and Longevity (Renshou Dian), with the name derived from *The Analects of Confucius* — "the benevolent enjoy longevity." ② This was where Empress Dowager Cixi and Emperor Guangxu handled court affairs and received foreign diplomats during their stay in the Summer Palace. As such, it was the Summer Palace's main government building.

B: Where are we heading for next?

A: ③ We are heading for the living quarters, composed of the Hall of Jade Ripples, the Grand Theatre and the Hall of Happiness and Longevity. This way, please.

B: The Grand Theatre? Is it where the emperor enjoyed Beijing Opera?

A: Yes. It is a 21-meter-high, 17-meter-wide, three-storey grand theatre. A deep well and five ponds supply water for special sound effects. It is said that approximately 1.6 million *liang* of silver was spent to build it in celebration of the 63rd birthday of Empress Dowager Cixi!

B: Unbelievable!

A: Here is the Hall of Happiness and Longevity, which was rebuilt in 1889. Empress Dowager Cixi lived here from April to October every year during the rest of her lifetime. ④ She regarded it as the place for avoiding summer heat and providing for the aged.

A: We are here now in the beautiful scenic quarter of the garden, where the emperor and his concubines enjoyed their leisure time. The main features of this quarter are the Kunming Lake and the Longevity Hill.

B: How large the lake is! What is the fragrant smell? So refreshing!

A: It's from the lotus beyond there. Kunming Lake is a half manmade and half natural lake, covering 3/4 of the Summer Palace, so it becomes the main scenic spot in the Summer Palace.

B: The emperors really knew how to enjoy life! Can we go riding the dragon boat?

A: Yes, of course. We'll have to take a short walk to the dock. Along the way, we can enjoy the beauty of the Long Corridor, or the Painted Walkway. It is the longest walkway in the Chinese gardens with altogether over 14,000 traditional Chinese paintings on the beams and crossbeams.

B: What a fabulous gallery of art! I may need plenty of time to admire the artistry here.

A: Sure. Take your time. (568 words)

Difficult Sentences

① Borrowing scenes from surrounding landscapes, it radiates not only the grandeur of an imperial garden but also the beauty of nature, in a seamless combination that best illustrates the guiding principle of traditional Chinese garden design: "The works of men should match the works of Heaven."
运用"借景"手法,颐和园不仅闪烁着皇家园林的恢宏气势,也散发着自然风光的旖旎。人工建筑与自然景观浑然一体,高度体现了中国园林"虽由人作,宛自天开"的造园准则。

② This was where Empress Dowager Cixi and Emperor Guangxu handled court affairs and received foreign diplomats during their stay in the Summer Palace.
慈禧太后和光绪皇帝驻跸颐和园时就在这里处理朝政,接见外国使臣。

③ We are heading for the living quarters, composed of the Hall of Jade Ripples, the Grand Theatre and the Hall of Happiness and Longevity.
我们接下来要参观的是生活区,主要建筑有玉澜堂、大戏楼和乐寿堂。

④ She regarded it as the place for avoiding summer heat and providing for the aged.
她视此处为消暑和颐养天年的好地方。

Text 4 Sacred Mountains of China: Four Great Mountains of Buddhism

Majestic mountains with tranquil ambience are all over China. These mountains mystify every visitor, and those who desire to live in these mountains develop the natural instinct for the love of nature and life itself. Monks, sages and holy men have been fascinated by these mountains which are very favorable for spiritual pursuit.

There are nine sacred mountains in China, including five Taoist sacred mountains and four Buddhist sacred mountains, each of which is spectacularly beautiful and contains at least one temple that is an important place of pilgrimage. ① So important are these mountains in Chinese religion that the very word for pilgrimage comes from the expression "paying respect to a holy mountain."

Each Buddhist sacred mountain is associated with a bodhisattva — an enlightened being who has postponed nirvana to help others gain enlightenment. The four mountains are:

NORTH: Wutai Mountain

Wutai Mountain (literally "Five Plateau Mountain"), also known as Qingliang Mountain, located in Shanxi, China, is one of the Four Sacred Mountains in Chinese Buddhism. The mountain is home to many of China's most important monasteries and temples. Mount Wutai's cultural heritage consists of 53 sacred monasteries.

② Famous for its time-honored history in temple establishment and the large scale, it is crowned as the first place of the four greatest Buddhist mountains. Mount Wutai is viewed as the place of practice of the Bodhisattva of Wisdom, Manjusri or Wenshu in Chinese. Mount Wutai also has an enduring relationship with Tibetan Buddhism.

WEST: Emei Mountain

Emei Mountain, a World Natural and Cultural Heritage in China, is located in Emeishan City of Sichuan province. It is in the upstream section of the Yangtze River. At 3,099 meters, Mt. Emei is the highest of the Four Sacred Buddhist Mountains of China. The patron bodhisattva of Emei is Samantabhadra, known in Chinese as Puxian. 16th and 17th century sources alluded to the practice of martial arts in the monasteries of Mount Emei as the place of origin for Chinese boxing[1].

SOUTH: Jiuhua Mountain

Jiuhua Mountain is located in Qingyang County in Anhui province and is famous for its rich landscape and ancient temples. It is a top-class attraction all around the world and an important international Buddhist holy land. Since the Han Dynasty, this famous mountain has accumulated so many splendid cultural and religious legacies that it has become the famous mountain of landscape, history, culture and Buddhism. It is considered the Land of Buddha and Lotus.

Many of the mountain's shrines and temples are dedicated to Ksitigarbha, known in Chinese as Dìzàng, who is a bodhisattva and protector of souls in hell according to Mahayana Buddhist tradition.

EAST: Putuo Mountain

Putuo Mountain is on the Zhoushan Islands, which comprise 1390 islands. Putuo Mountain is the first group of national key places of interest, generally called Buddhist Heaven on the sea and the Holy Land on the South Sea. ③ The immortal mountains in clouds and waters offer travelers the feeling of mystery, strangeness, and sanctity. It is famous in Chinese Buddhism for it is considered the bodhimanda of Avalokitesvara (Guan Yin), a revered bodhisattva in many parts of East Asia. (529 words)

---

1 峨眉武术与少林、武当并列为中华武术的三大流派。其中，峨眉武术距今已有2500年历史，是历史悠久、创派最早的武术流派，比少林武术早1000年，比武当早1600年，是中华武术的发源地。

Difficult Sentences

① So important are these mountains in Chinese religion that the very word for pilgrimage comes from the expression "paying respect to a holy mountain."
这些山在中国宗教界极负盛名，在中国朝圣就称为"拜山"。

② Famous for its time-honored history in temple establishment and the large scale, it is crowned as the first place of the four greatest Buddhist mountains.
五台山因其寺庙历史之悠久，修建规模之宏大被冠以四大佛教名山之首的美誉。

③ The immortal mountains in clouds and waters offer travelers the feeling of mystery, strangeness, and sanctity.
云雾缭绕、烟波荡漾中伫立的仙山缥缈，让游人顿生神秘、虚幻和圣洁之感。

 *Exercises 2*

Task 1 Listening Comprehension

Directions: *Listen to the Situational Dialogue in Text 3, read the four choices marked A, B, C and D, and decide which is the best answer.*

1. Which one is not included in the four famous gardens in China?

    A. The Summer Palace.

    B. The Humble Administrator's Garden.

    C. The Chengde Summer Resort.

    D. The Garden of Harmonious Interests.

2. The guiding principle of traditional Chinese garden art is "_____."

    A. natural scenery should be included

    B. the works of men are inferior to the works of Heaven

    C. the works of men should match the works of Heaven

    D. men should spare no effort to imitate the natural scenery

3. From which Chinese Classics does the Hall of Benevolence and Longevity derive its name?

    A. *The Great Learning*.

    B. *The Analects of Confucius*.

    C. *The Doctrine of the Mean*.

    D. *Mencius*.

4. Which building is the main government building in the Summer Palace?

    A. The Hall of Benevolence and Longevity.

    B. The Hall of Happiness and Longevity.

    C. The Hall of Jade Ripples.

    D. The Hall of Dispelling Clouds.

5. What will the tourist be doing at the end of the conversation?

    A. Appreciating the paintings on the Long Corridor.

B. Taking a short cut to the dock.
C. Riding the dragon boat.
D. Painting the Long Corridor.

Task 2 Spot Dictation

Directions: *In this section you will hear the passage taken from Text 4 three times. When the passage is read for the first time, you should listen carefully for its general idea. When the passage is read for the second time, you are required to fill in the blanks with the exact words you have just heard. Finally, when the passage is read for the third time, you should check what you have written.*

Majestic mountains with tranquil ambience (氛围) are (1)_____ China. These mountains (2)_____ every visitor, and those who desire to live in these mountain develop the natural (3)_____ for the love of nature and life itself. Monks, sages and holy men (4)_____ these mountains which are very (5)_____ for spiritual pursuit.

There are nine sacred mountains in China, including five Taoist sacred mountains and four Buddhist sacred mountains, each of which is (6)_____ beautiful and contains at least one (7)_____ that is an important place of pilgrimage. So important are these mountains in Chinese (8)_____ that the very word for pilgrimage (9)_____ the expression "paying respect to a holy mountain."

Each Buddhist sacred mountain is associated with a bodhisattva (菩萨) —an enlightened being who has postponed nirvana (涅槃) to help others gain (10)_____. The four mountains are: Wutai Mountain, Emei Mountain, Jiuhua Mountain, and Putuo Mountain.

Task 3 Short Answer Questions

Directions: *Read Text 3 and Text 4, and then answer the following questions briefly.*
1. Did the Summer Palace only provide entertainment for the royal members?
2. What do you know about the Kunming Lake?
3. Which of the four mountains bears close relationship with Tibetan Buddhism?
4. Who is the patron bodhisattva of Putuo Mountain?
5. Which mountain is the highest of the Four Sacred Mountains?

Task 4 Translation

Directions: *Translate the following passage from Chinese into English.*
颐和园是迄今为止保存最完好、最大的中国皇家园林。它位于北京，距市中心10千米。颐和园是中国经典园林的佼佼者，享有国际盛誉。该园于1924年向公众开放。1998年，颐和园被联合国教科文组织列入世界遗产名录。颐和园的两大主要景区是万寿山和昆明湖。昆明湖是一个半天然，半人工湖，占颐和园总面积的四分之三。万寿山脚下有一条长728米的画廊，是中国园林中最长的画廊，其梁柱上绘有中国传统画作共14000余幅。

Words and Expressions for "Land of Splendor"

Text 1	
emblem	*n.* 象征，标记
legendary	*adj.* 传说的；传奇的
loess	*n.* 黄土
the Cradle of the Chinese Civilization	中华文明的摇篮
overture	*n.* 序曲
birthplace	*n.* 发祥地
matriarchal culture	母系氏族文化
Loess Plateau	黄土高原
Yushu Tibetan Prefecture	玉树藏族自治州
inhospitable	*adj.* 不适于居住的
Genghis Khan	成吉思汗
Ordos	鄂尔多斯
must-see	*n.* 必须游览的景点
nomadic pastoral life	游牧民族的田园生活
dugout	*n.* 窑洞
mausoleum	*n.* 陵墓
Buddhist grottoes	佛教石窟
recreational park	休闲公园
breathtaking	*adj.* 非常激动人心的；惊人的
Pota Pagoda	繁塔
Shanxi-Shaanxi-Gansu Guild Hall	山陕甘会馆
Remains of Mosque of Judaism	犹太教清真寺遗址
Text 2	
military defence project	军事防御工程
successive	*adj.* 连续的；相继的
fortification	*n.* 防御工事
ducal states	诸侯国
plunder	*v.* （尤指战乱时用武力）抢劫；掠夺
the nomadic peoples	游牧民族
mountain ranges	山脉
ward off	抵挡；防止
harassment	*n.* 骚扰；烦扰
went to ruin through years of neglect	年久失修

续表

intervening	adj. 发生于其间的；介于中间的
renovation	n. 翻新；翻修；修整
rammed	adj. 夯实的
imposing	adj. 壮观的；使人印象深刻的
rampart	n.（城堡或城市周围的）城墙；壁垒
gallop	v.（马等）飞奔；奔驰；疾驰
abreast	adv. 并列；并排；并肩
embrasure	n. 斜面门（或窗）洞（两侧向内渐宽）
peep-hole	n. 窥视孔
aperture	n. 光圈；缝隙；小孔
gargoyle	n.（建筑物的）滴水嘴；滴水兽
parapet	n. 防护矮墙
contour	n. 外形；轮廓
quarter	v. 给……提供食宿
garrison	n. 卫戍部队；守备部队
merge	v. 相融；渐渐消失在某物中
bonfire	n. 篝火；营火
relay	v. 转发（信息、消息等）
collision and exchanges	碰撞与交流
unparalleled	adj. 无与伦比的；空前的；无比的
Text 3	
the best preserved	保存最完好的
Chengde Summer Resort	承德避暑山庄
Humble Administrator's Garden	拙政园
Lingering Garden	留园
resemble	v. 与……相像，类似于
Hall of Supreme Harmony	太和殿
The Analects of Confucius	《论语》
artistry	n. 艺术之性质；技艺
Hall of Benevolence and Longevity	仁寿殿
Longevity Hill	万寿山
Hall of Jade Ripples	玉澜堂
Hall of Happiness and Longevity	乐寿堂
Garden of Virtue and Harmony	德和园大戏楼

续表

Hall of Dispelling Clouds	排云殿
Tower of Buddhist Incense	佛香阁
Garden of Harmonious Interests	谐趣园
Kunming Lake	昆明湖
Long Corridor	长廊
17-Arch Bridge	十七孔桥
Bronze Ox	铜牛
Wenchang Gallery	文昌院
Pavilion of Bright Scenery	景明楼
Hall of Listening to the Orioles	听鹂馆
Suzhou Street	苏州街
Text 4	
majestic	*adj.* 宏伟的；壮丽的；庄重的
tranquil ambience	宁静的氛围
mystify	*v.* 使神秘化
spiritual pursuit	精神追求
pilgrimage	*n.* 朝觐，朝圣
bodhisattva	*n.* 菩萨
nirvana	*n.* 涅槃
monastery	*n.* 修道院，寺院
cultural heritage	文化遗产
its time-honored history	悠久历史
is crowned as	被冠以……之名
martial arts	武术
the earliest extant reference (to sth.)	现存最早的记载
place of origin	发源地
legacy	*n.* 遗产；遗赠
Mahayana Buddhism	大乘佛教
bodhimanda	*n.* 道场
revered	*adj.* 备受尊敬的

Key to Exercises

Exercises 1

Task 1 Short Answer Questions

1. Its convenient location.

2. It is famous for being the historic Communist headquarters and for having the Mausoleum of the Yellow Emperor.

3. Seven provinces and two autonomous regions.

4. It was constructed as a military defence project to ward off harassments from the nomadic peoples in the north.

5. They employed a signal system consisting of beacon towers on the Wall itself and on mountain tops within sight of the Wall.

Task 2 Reading Comprehension

1. unparalleled   2. construction   3. renovations   4. legacy   5. preserved
6. ward   7. collision   8. hardships   9. consolidation   10. anthem

Task 3 Translation

The Yellow River, with a length of 5464km, is the second-longest river in China after the Yangtze River. The river rises/originates in Qinghai province on the Plateau of Tibet. It flows eastward through/crosses six other provinces and two autonomous regions in its course and finally empties into the Bohai Sea. The Yellow River is called the "Mother River" of the Chinese People, and is also referred to as "the Cradle of Chinese Civilization", as its basin was the birthplace of ancient Chinese civilization. It was also the most prosperous and populous region in early Chinese history. Till the Song Dynasty and Yuan Dynasty, the Yellow River basin had always been the center of China's economy and had developed the most advanced civilization in the world then.

Task 4 Writing
Sample Writing

Natural and Cultural Heritage Preservation in China

With changes taking place in social and economic conditions, the sites have met with many problems such as natural disasters, over-exposure to human activities, pollution and overdevelopment for economic gains. To protect our precious cultural and natural heritages, as well as to preserve our historical, social and cultural dignity, our government and its people have been making great efforts in this field.

China joined the World Heritage Convention in 1985, which means China accepts the value and aims of the convention. In the process of applying for world heritage status and preserving and protecting its own world heritage sites, the concept of heritage protection in China is gradually developing and progressing. To protect its natural heritages more effectively, the Chinese government has legislated laws—Natural Heritage Preservation Law. And management regulations are strictly enforced. What's more, the banks have given priorities to loans for heritage preservation, enabling experts to research on more advanced technology.

Any type of heritage can only be properly developed when its value is sufficiently appreciated. When people notice and recognize the value of these heritages, they will start to protect them and save them from destructive development. So, the government and experts are committed to arouse public awareness and to educate citizens of the importance of preservation. Nowadays, there are many non-governmental organizations dedicated to this noble cause. Some of China's wealthiest business leaders are coming together in an attempt to rescue part of their country's natural heritage from extinction. (251 words)

Exercises 2

Task 1 Listening Comprehension
1. D   2. C   3. B   4. A   5. A

Task 2 Spot Dictation
1. all over   2. mystify   3. instinct   4. have been fascinated by
5. favorable   6. spectacularly 7. temple   8. religion
9. comes from   10. enlightenment

Task 3 Short Answer Questions
1. No, the emperors handled court affairs and received foreign diplomats during their stay in the Summer Palace.
2. Kunming Lake is a half manmade and half natural lake, covering 3/4 of the Summer Palace, so it becomes the main scenic spot in the Summer Palace.
3. Wutai Mountain.
4. Avalokitesvara (Guan Yin), a revered bodhisattva in many parts of East Asia.
5. Emei Mountain.

Task 4 Translation
The Summer Palace is up to now the best preserved and the largest imperial garden in China. Situated in Beijing, it is 10 kilometers from the central city. It is China's leading classical garden which enjoys a worldwide reputation. The Summer Palace was opened to the public in 1924 and included in the UNESCO World Heritage List in 1998. The two main elements of the garden are the Longevity Hill and the Kunming Lake. The Kunming Lake is a half manmade and half natural lake, taking up three quarters of the garden. At the foot of the Longevity Hill is the 728-meter-long Painted Walkway which is the longest walkway in the Chinese gardens with altogether over 14,000 traditional Chinese paintings on the beams and crossbeams.

Unit Chinese Food Culture

> **导读**
>
> 本单元旨在通过对中国饮食文化的介绍，使学生能够运用所学中国饮食文化知识及相关的英语表达进行跨文化交流，弘扬中华饮食文化。

Before You Start

While you are preparing for this unit, think about the following questions:

1. What do you know about Lao Zi and Daoism(or Taoism), Confucius and Confucianism? What are their major philosophical ideas? How do these ideas influence the Chinese people in their culinary culture?
2. What do you know about Chinese food? If a foreign friend visits your hometown, how would you tell him/her about the food there?

Section A Reading and Writing

Text 1 The Principles of Chinese Cuisine

Characteristic features of Chinese cuisine are closely related to Chinese culture. Food is part of the way of life, strongly influenced by the two early philosophies of Daoism (Taoism) and Confucianism.

Both Lao Zi (Lao Tzu, ca. 571 BC—471 BC), the founder of Daoism, and Confucius (551 BC—479 BC) lived and taught during the late Zhou Dynasty. It was the Daoist school that developed the hygienic and nutritional science of food, while Confucianism was more concerned with the art of cooking.

You will have noticed that a Chinese dish is usually made up of more than one ingredient; this is because when a single item is cooked on its own, it lacks contrast and therefore lacks harmony. For centuries, Chinese cooks have understood the importance of the harmonious balance in blending different flavors. ① The principle of blending complementary or contrasting colors, flavors and textures is based on the ancient Daoist school of philosophy known as the *yin-yang* principle, which practically governs all aspects of Chinese life, and has been the guiding principle for all Chinese cooks. ② Consciously or unconsciously, every Chinese cook, from the housewife to the professional chef, works to the *yin-yang* principle, i.e. the harmonious balance and contrast in the conspicuous placement of different colors, aroma, flavors, shapes and textures, achieved by varying the ingredients, seasonings, cutting techniques, and cooking methods.

Another characteristic of Chinese cuisine is the Chinese belief that all foods are also medicines—the overriding idea is that the kind of food one eats is closely related to one's health. This Daoist approach classifies all foods into those that possess the *yin*, meaning "cool" quality, and those that possess the *yang*, or "hot" quality. When the *yin-yang* forces in the body are not balanced, illness results. To combat this disorder, it is necessary to eat foods that will redress the balance. This belief was documented in the third century BC, at the beginning of herbal medicine and the recognition of the link between nutrition and health, and it is still a dominant concept in Chinese culture today.

The *yin-yang* principle can also be seen in the basic dualism of nature: *yin* is feminine, dark, cool and passive; *yang*, in contrast, is masculine, bright, hot and active. But unlike the dualism of the Western world, in which good and evil are in perpetual conflict, *yin* and *yang* complement each other and form a harmonious pair.

③ Over the years, as the *yin-yang* principle developed along dualist lines, it was combined with the "five elements" concept of the Naturalist school of thought, which held that nature is made up of various combinations of five elements of nature: metal, wood, water, fire and earth. The parallel to the four elements of the ancient Greeks—earth, fire, air and water—is striking. The number five has always played an important part in Chinese food culture. Not only do we have the famous five-spice powder but we also have the five flavors seen as fundamental to Chinese cooking: sweet, sour, bitter, hot and salty. The earliest book on medicine, Huang Di Nei Jing[1] (*Huang Di's Canon of Internal Medicine*), written over two thousand years ago, proposed that the body needed five flavors to live, five grains for nourishment, five fruits for support, five animals for benefit, and five vegetables for energy. (560 words)
(*Based on INTERNATIONAL CUISINE—China, Hodder & Stoughton.*)

Difficult Sentences

① The principle of blending complementary or contrasting colors, flavors and textures is based on the ancient Daoist school of philosophy known as the *yin-yang* principle.
色、香、味相互补充或对比鲜明的原则以古代道家哲学的阴阳法则为基础。

---

1 《黄帝内经》是中国传统医学四大经典著作(《黄帝内经》《难经》《伤寒杂病论》《神农本草经》)之一，是我国医学宝库中现存成书最早的一部医学典籍。一般认为成书于春秋战国时期。

② Consciously or unconsciously, every Chinese cook, from the housewife to the professional chef, works to the *yin-yang* principle, i.e. the harmonious balance and contrast in the conspicuous placement of different colors, aroma, flavors, shapes and textures, achieved by varying the ingredients, seasonings, cutting techniques, and cooking methods.

无论是家庭主妇还是职业厨师，每位中国烹饪者都会有意无意地按照阴阳法则烹饪食物。也就是说，通过使用各种不同的食材、调料、变化的刀工和烹饪方法，使不同颜色、香气、风味、形状和口感的食物明显达到和谐的平衡与对比。

③ Over the years, as the *yin-yang* principle developed along dualist lines, it was combined with the "five elements" concept of the Naturalist school of thought, which held that nature is made up of various combinations of five elements of nature: metal, wood, water, fire and earth.

许多年来，阴阳法则随着二元学说一起发展，它结合了自然主义学派的五行概念，即自然是由金、木、水、火、土五个要素通过不同形式的组合构成的。

Text 2 Regional Cuisines

CCTV's documentary, "A Bite of China," which tells an amazing story of the Chinese cuisine, introduces different regional varieties and shows the hard work and profound artistry hidden behind each and every dish, has become a hot topic in China's blogosphere in recent years.

China has a wide variety of cuisines in different regions, and among which the most influential, representative and socially acknowledged are Lu, Chuan, Yue, Min, Su, Zhe, Xiang and Hui cuisines, often noted as the "Eight Major Cuisines," of which Yue, Lu, Su and Chuan cusines are the best known.

A cuisine cannot exist without its long history and unique cooking. It is influenced by the natural geography, climate, products, resources, and eating habits. ① Someone said Su and Zhe cuisines are like the elegant beauties of the south, Lu and Hui cuisines are like strong earthy men of the north, Xiang and Min cuisines are like romantic gentlemen, and Chuan and Yue cuisines are like elites rich of talents.

Yue (Cantonese)

Cantonese cuisine originated in the Han Dynasty and enjoys extremely good reputation home and abroad for its unique types of dishes and special charm. Its prominence outside China is due to the great numbers of early Guangdong emigrants. When people in the West speak of Chinese food, they usually mean Cantonese food. With the advantages of all delicacies from all over the country, Cantonese cuisine has gradually formed its own characteristics—using a wide variety of ingredients, offering food of all tastes, shapes and colors, good at changing, and serving light food in summer and autumn, and strong and mellow food in winter and spring. Cantonese style features fresh and delicious tastes with a clear and fragrant smell.

Cantonese snacks are peculiar about ingredients, some sweet and some salty, enjoying the reputation of "100 kinds of snacks having 100 tastes and 100 shapes."

Lu (Shandong)

Shandong cuisine is considered as the most influential in Chinese cuisine, with the majority of the culinary styles in China having developed from it. Nowadays, schools of cuisine in North China, such as those of Beijing, Tianjin, and Northeast, are all branches of Shandong cuisine. Also, the typical dishes in most part of North China households' meals are prepared in simplified Shandong methods. With a long history, Shandong cuisine once formed an important part of the imperial cuisine. It is featured by a variety of cooking techniques and seafood. Various Shandong snacks are also worth trying.

Su (Huaiyang)

Su cuisine is derived from the native cooking styles of the region surrounding the lower reaches of the Huai River and the Yangtze River, and centered upon the cities of Huai'an, Yangzhou and Zhenjiang in Jiangsu province. In general, its texture is characterized as soft. Other features include the strict selection of ingredients according to the  seasons, emphasis on the matching color and shape of each dish and emphasis on using soup to improve the flavor.

Although sometimes simply called Su cuisine, the most popular and prestigious style of it is Huaiyang cuisine, which tends to have a sweet side to it and is almost never spicy. The way that ingredient is cut is pivotal to its cooking and its final taste. Pork, fresh water fish and other aquatic creatures serve as the meat base to most dishes.

Chuan (Sichuan)

Chuan cuisine, which is primarily based on Chengdu and Chongqing dishes, is the most widely served cuisine in China and enjoys a high reputation both home and abroad. ② Chuan cuisine focuses on the refined selection of raw materials, the dimensions, the harmonious layout and the  sharp contrasting taste and colors. It is composed of seven basic flavors: sour, pungent, hot, sweet, bitter, aromatic and salty, and win universal praise for its hotness, sourness and numbness produced from the delicate use of pepper or chili.

The ingredients used are great in variety, including poultry, pork, beef, fish, vegetables and tofu. ③ The methods of cooking vary according to the texture required. Stir frying, steaming and braising are the most widely used. (671 words)

Difficult Sentences

① Someone said Su and Zhe cuisines are like the elegant beauties of the South, Lu and Hui cuisines are like the strong earthy men of the north; Xiang and Min cuisines are like romantic gentlemen, and Chuan and Yue cuisines are like elites rich of talents.
有人说苏、浙菜系就像婉约优雅的江南美女，鲁、徽菜系像强健朴实的北方男人，湘菜和闽菜像浪漫的绅士，川粤菜则像才华出众的精英人士。

② Chuan cuisine focuses on the refined selection of raw materials, the dimensions, the harmonious layout and the sharp contrasting taste and colors.
川菜注重食材的精选，切块的尺寸，摆盘的和谐，以及味道和色彩的强烈对比。

③ The methods of cooking vary according to the texture required. Stir frying, steaming and braising are the most widely used.
烹调方法根据食材质地的不同需求而变化，最广泛使用的方式是炒、蒸和炖。

Exercises 1

Task 1 Short Answer Questions

Directions: *Read Text 1 and Text 2 and then answer the following questions briefly.*

1. Why is a Chinese dish usually made up of more than one ingredient?
2. Which principle does every Chinese cook follow in making a dish?
3. What is the difference between the dualism of the Western world and *yin-yang* principle?
4. What are the five elements of the Naturalist school of thought?
5. What are the "Eight Major Cuisines" in China?

Task 2 Reading Comprehension

Part A

Directions: *Complete the following five sentences with the proper forms of the words given in the brackets.*

1. All theories _____ (origin) from practice and in turn serve practice.
2. Gardeners _____ (class) plants according to their life-duration and frost susceptibility.
3. If we were designing a house, we'd be _____ (concern) with how the rooms should be positioned with respect to each other.
4. The concept of building a _____ (harmony) society has rooted deeply in people's mind.
5. He is in many ways _____ (character) of the age in which he lived.

Part B

Directions: *In this section, you are going to read a passage with five statements attached to it. Each statement contains information given in one of the paragraphs. Identify the paragraph from which the information is derived. Each paragraph is marked with a letter.*

Beijing Traditional Snacks Facing Challenges

A) Beijing has been the capital of China for centuries, so its cuisine is influenced by culinary traditions from all over China. The tradition that influenced Beijing cuisine is the Chinese imperial cuisine that originated from yùshànfáng, or the "Emperor's Kitchen," which referred to the cooking facilities inside the Forbidden City, where thousands of cooks from different parts of China showed their best culinary skills to please the imperial family and officials. Therefore, it is sometimes difficult to determine the actual origin of a dish.

B) What are the traditional snacks that Beijingers have been enjoying? Beijing boasts a variety of traditional snacks which are imbued with local culture. For example, snacks like Aiwowo, an imperial candy, is a sugar-filled ball of glutinous rice and a favorite of the Empress Cixi; Lvdagunr (Rolling Donkey), glutinous rice rolls stuffed with red bean paste, and Wandouhuang (Pea Flour Cake), made from a mixture of white peas and sugar, date back to Ming Dynasty (1368—1644) and are already listed as intangible cultural heritage in several districts in Beijing.

C) Since foods that originated in Beijing are often snacks rather than main courses, and they are typically sold by small shops or street vendors. The famous snack streets include Wangfujing, Jiumen ("nine gates") snack center at Shichahai, Niu Jie, Menkuang Hutong and the narrow hutongs of Dashilar. But the number has dwindled drastically, and waning popularity has meant fewer and fewer shops sell authentic Beijing-style snacks.

D) According to statistics by the Beijing Snack Food Development Association released last year, traditional Beijing snacks have declined sharply from 600 varieties at their peak to about 100 today, and the average age of authentic inheritors of their craft are mostly over 70 years old. Moreover, the craft of traditional snacks is likely to die out as the rent is increasing and its financial prospects are diminishing.

E) Young people are unwilling to learn the craftsmanship, as they cannot make enough money. However, the most severe challenge to Beijing's culinary classics is the increasing number of non-traditional stores, which pose a threat to the reputation of traditional Beijing snacks. Some of the vendors or stores who claim they are time-honored Beijing snack maker just copy the ingredients and don't know the right way to make the snacks.

F) Traditional Beijing snacks are as important as the Great Wall or Summer Palace. It's not only a part of cultural heritage, but the embodiment of a city. But as the city develops into an international metropolis, many of these time-honored brands are being crowded out of the market. The high ingredient costs and low-selling prices are eating away their profits. It is time for the government and public to take measures to protect this intangible cultural heritage.

(　) 1. Beijing-style snacks are usually sold by small shops or sellers outside on the streets.
(　) 2. Traditional Beijing snacks are on the verge of extinction since its profits are shrinking and real inheritors are getting old.
(　) 3. The high ingredient costs and low-selling prices are eating away their profits.
(　) 4. It is not easy to identify the origin of Beijing cuisine.
(　) 5. Younger generations are reluctant to learn the crafts of Beijing snacks because they cannot bring them enough profits.

Task 3　Translation

Directions: *Translate the following passage from Chinese into English.*

中国菜通常由不止一种原料做成，这是因为用料单一菜就会缺少对比，因而很难达到和谐。通过使用各种不同的食材、调料、变化的刀工和烹饪方法，使不同颜色、香气、风味、形状和口感的食物达到和谐的平衡和对比。阴阳原则支配着中国人生活的方方面面，也是中国厨师做饭的指导性原则。所有的食物也是药材，一个人吃的食物与其健康息息相关。当阴阳的力量在体内不平衡时人就会生病。现在越来越多的人已经认识到营养与健康之间的关系。

Task 4　Writing

Direction: *The documentary "A Bite of China" offers a deep insight into the geographical, historical and cultural dimensions of what Chinese people eat. Watch the 2nd episode of "A Bite of China I" (the Story of Staple Food) and write a research report focusing on the following two points: (1) What are the representative staple foods in different regions of China; (2) What are the geographical, historical and cultural elements related to these typical regional foods.*

Section B　Listening and Speaking

Text 3　Situational Dialogue: Beijing Roast Duck

(*A: Waiter;　B & C: Guests*)

A: Good evening. ① We cater to both Chinese and western tastes. Which would you prefer, Chinese or western?

B: We'll have Chinese food for a change today. Could you tell us what kind of Chinese food you serve here?

A: We serve Cantonese, Sichuan, Shanghai and Beijing cuisine.

B: Could you tell me about their different features?

A: Generally, Cantonese food is light and clear, Sichuan food is hot and spicy, Shanghai food is a little greasy, while Beijing food is salty and tasty.

B: We'd like to try some Beijing food. Could you make some suggestions?

A: Certainly. The Beijing Roast Duck is a Beijing specialty. It's very delicious and its skin is really crispy.

B: ② Sounds so inviting! We'll order for two.

A: You can have a whole duck or half of it. I think a half duck is enough for two persons. Is that all right?

B: OK.

A: Your Roast Duck, gentlemen.

C: Could you show us how to eat it, please?

A: Certainly. First, hold a pancake in your hand and paint a few splashes of the bean sauce on the pancake with some scallion…like this.Next, add a few pieces of the duck meat with your chopsticks. Finally, roll the pancake up and enjoy it!

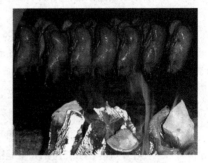

C: Let's have a try. Is that right?

A: Yes. Perfect!

B: So tender and crispy! I've never tasted anything like this. How is it made?

A: The preparation is a bit complicated. ③ First, ducks must be split open, dressed, scalded and dried. In the process of roasting, we use fruit tree branches as firewood to lend more flavor to the duck. Besides, a steady temperature must be maintained in the oven and ducks must be rotated so that they are evenly roasted.

B: How long does it take to roast the duck?

A: About 50 minutes. And when the skin turns crispy and golden brown, the duck is done.

B & C: How interesting!

A: Would you like any vegetables or soup?

B: Yes, please. What would you recommend?

A: ④ Season Vegetables in Oyster Sauce and Mushroom Soup.

B: OK, They'll be served soon.

A: Would you care for anything to drink? We have Mao-tai. It's a real Chinese specialty. It's strong but won't get into your head.

B & C: It's terrific! We'll order one bottle of Mao-tai. Next time we'll invite more friends to taste it. (414 words)

 Difficult Sentences

① We cater to both Chinese and western tastes.
　　句中cater to的意思是"供应……饮食服务"。

② Sounds so inviting!
　　此句省略了主语That (It), inviting意思是"诱人的，吸引人的"。

③ First, ducks must be split open, dressed, scalded and dried.
　　首先，要把鸭子开膛，褪毛，烫皮，晾干。

④ Seasonal vegetables in Oyster Sauce and Mushroom Soup.
蚝油时蔬和蘑菇汤。

Related Expressions and Sentences

1. Our restaurant mainly serves Cantonese cuisine. 本餐厅主营粤菜。

2. When you are in China, do as the Chinese do. Use the chopsticks. 到了中国，就要入乡随俗。用筷子吧。

3. How about our specialty Thick Corn Soup and Mapo Tofu, Sir? They must suit your taste. 先生，来一个本店特色菜玉米羹和麻婆豆腐怎么样？我想它们比较适合先生您的口味。

4. These are typical Beijing dishes. 这些是地道的北京菜。

5. Would you like large or small portions? 你是要大份的还是小份的？

6. According to the Chinese practice, we serve the food first and then the soup. 按中国习俗，我们先上菜，后上汤。

7. Chinese cookery places great emphasis on three elements: color, aroma and taste. The color of a dish has to be satisfying to the eye, and the balance of colors is kept in mind during its preparation. 中国烹饪讲究色、香、味三要素。菜的色彩要悦目，做菜需要色彩的搭配。

8. The Chinese cuisine is based on five tastes: sour, sweet, bitter, spicy and salty. 中国菜以五味为主，即酸、甜、苦、辣、咸。

9. Generally, Cantonese food is light and clear; Sichuan food is hot and spicy, Shanghai food is a little greasy while Beijing food is salty and tasty. 一般说来，粤菜清淡，川菜麻辣，上海菜重油，而北京菜咸香。

10. We have Maotai. It's a real Chinese specialty. It's strong but won't get into your head. 我们有茅台酒。这是真正的中国特产，酒劲大，却不上头。

Text 4 A Tour Guide Commentary on Beijing Snacks

Beijing has a time-honored history of producing various kinds of snacks. With strong local flavors, Beijing's snacks attract almost all visitors. If you want to get a feel for the life of a Beijing resident, you can start by walking around the city streets, tasting some traditional Beijing snacks. There are approximately more than 200 of them and they fall into three varieties: Han, Hui and court snacks.

Here are a few of the most popular:

Mung Bean Milk (Douzhi) is probably the most famous Beijing snack. ① It is actually the fluid remnants of the mung bean noodle making process. It tastes mostly sour with a tinge of sweetness, and has a peculiar odor—it's definitely an acquired taste. First-timers often drink mung bean milk together with Chinese-style pickles, which locals say makes it easier to go down. Because of its low price, it used to be welcomed by the majority of Beijingers.

Another famous snack, **Sticky Rice Balls (Aiwowo)**, is a court snack. As white as snow, this delicacy is made of sticky rice. The rice is first steamed then pounded and shaped into a ball. It is then given fillings, which might be sesame and white sugar, pea-flour, Chinese date paste or some other treats. ② Flexible in consistency and with a distinctive smooth texture, this dainty snack became a favorite of imperial and noble families during the Ming Dynasty (1368—1644). It is said that it came to be called Ai Wo Wo (emperor's special) because one particular emperor loved it so much.

Pea Flour Cake (Wandouhuang), made with white peas, is a favorite springtime snack, and was very popular among members of the imperial court. ③ A good pea flour cake should have a loose consistency; the taste should be refreshing, but not too sweet.

Luzhu

If you are not allergic to the viscus of animals, you can try to have some Luzhu. It is made of the tharm and stomach of the pigs. Though it sounds disgusting, it is in fact very delicious.

Most Beijing snacks can be found around Qianmen Gate, ④ but many Beijingers prefer to go to Longfusi[1] or Huguosi[2] Snack Streets to satisfy their snacking needs. In ancient times snack vendors would gather in the areas during temple fairs held on the eighth of every month (lunar calendar). Though the regular temple fairs ended long ago, bringing an end to the gathering of snack vendors, Beijingers say they have managed to recreate the tastes of the areas' past.

If all this talk of food is making you hungry, just get up and grab some of them. (448 words)

Difficult Sentences

① It is actually the fluid remnants of the mung bean noodle making process.
豆汁是用制造绿豆粉丝过程中剩余的液体残渣（发酵）做成的。

② Flexible in consistency and with a distinctive smooth texture, this dainty snack became a favorite of imperial and noble families during the Ming Dynasty.

1　北京隆福寺坐落在东四北大街西，始建于明代景泰三年（1425），清雍正九年重修。隆福寺在明代是京城唯一的番（喇嘛）、禅（和尚）同驻的寺院，清代成为完全的喇嘛庙。因坐落在东城，与护国寺相对，俗称"东庙"。

2　北京护国寺是北京八大寺庙之一，始建于元代。位于西城西四牌楼之北，护国寺街西口内路北。护国寺庙会与隆福寺庙会齐名，即所谓"东西二庙"之西庙。

（艾窝窝）这种精美小吃口感绵软细滑，味道独特，很快就成为明朝王公贵族们的最爱。

③ A good pea flour cake should have a loose consistency; the taste should be refreshing, but not too sweet.

好的豌豆黄应该是松软、爽口，而不甜腻。

④ ... but many Beijingers prefer to go to Longfusi or Huguosi Snack Streets to satisfy their snacking needs.

但许多北京人喜欢去隆福寺和护国寺小吃一条街去品尝北京小吃。

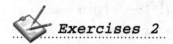

Exercises 2

Task 1 Listening Comprehension

Directions: *Listen to the Situational Dialogue in Text 3, read the four choices marked A, B, C and D, and decide which is the best answer.*

1. What does the guest order in the conversation?
   A. Western food.   B. Chinese food.
   C. American food.   D. Both A and B.
2. What are the characteristics of Shanghai food?
   A. Light and clear.   B. Hot and spicy.
   C. A little greasy.   D. Salty and tasty.
3. How many ducks does the waiter recommend to the guest?
   A. One duck.   B. One and a half duck.
   C. Half a duck.   D. More than one duck.
4. What is used as firewood to lend more flavor to the roasted duck?
   A. Fruit tree branches.   B. Coal and branches.
   C. Fruits and vegetables. D. Fruit and wine.
5. How long does it take to roast the duck?
   A. About 5 minutes.   B. About 15 minutes.
   C. About 25 minutes.   D. About 50 minutes.

Task 2 Spot Dictation

Directions: *In this section you will hear the passage based on Text 4 three times. When the passage is read for the first time, you should listen carefully for its general idea. When the passage is read for the second time, you are required to fill in the blanks with the exact words you have just heard. Finally, when the passage is read for the third time, you should check what you have written.*

Beijing has a time-honored history of (1)_____ various kinds of snacks. With strong local flavors, Beijing's snacks attract almost all visitors. If you want to get a feel for the life of a Beijing (2)_____, you can start by walking around the city streets, tasting some (3)_____ Beijing snacks. There are approximately more than 200 of them and they fall into three varieties: Han,

Hui and court snacks. Here are a few of the most popular:

Mung Bean Milk (Douzhi) is (4)_____ the most famous Beijing snack. It is actually the fluid remnants of the mung bean noodle making process. It tastes mostly sour with a tinge of sweetness, and has a peculiar odor. First-timers often drink mung bean milk together with Chinese-style pickles, which locals say makes it (5)_____ to go down. Because of its low price, it used to be welcomed by the majority of Beijingers.

Another famous snack, Sticky Rice Balls (Aiwowo), is a court snack. As white as snow, this (6)_____ is made of sticky rice. The rice is first steamed then pounded and (7)_____ into a ball. It is then given fillings (馅), which might be sesame and white sugar, pea-flour, Chinese date paste or some other treats.

Most Beijing snacks can be found around Qianmen Gate, but many Beijingers prefer to go Longfusi or Huguosi Snack Streets to satisfy their snacking needs. (8)_____ snack vendors would gather in the areas during temple fairs held on the eighth of every month (lunar calendar). Though the regular temple fairs ended long ago, (9)_____ to the gathering of snack vendors, Beijingers say they have (10)_____ recreate the tastes of the areas' past.

Task 3 Short Answer Questions

Directions: *Read Text 3 and Text 4, and then answer the following questions briefly.*

1. How could you guarantee that the duck is evenly roasted in the oven?
2. What is the typical feature of Mao-tai?
3. How many Beijing snacks are there and how could they be classified?
4. Why is Sticky Rice Balls named as Ai Wo Wo?
5. Where could you find most Beijing snacks?

Task 4 Translation

Directions: *Translate the following passage from Chinese into English.*

北京的小吃制作有着悠久的历史，具有浓郁的地方风味，吸引了几乎所有的游客。豆汁是北京最著名的小吃之一。它尝起来酸中带甜，有种特殊的香味。由于价格低廉，受到多数北京人的喜爱。另一种著名的小吃艾窝窝是宫廷小吃。它是一种由糯米制成的洁白如雪的美味。米先蒸再捣碎，做成球的形状。这种美味的小吃深受明朝皇室和贵族家庭的喜爱，据说艾窝窝曾是皇帝的特供。

Words and Expressions for Chinese Food Culture

Text 1	
Daoism	*n.* 道家（学派）
Confucianism	*n.* 儒家（学说）
hygienic	*adj.* 卫生的
complementary	*adj.* 互补的
texture	*n.* 质地；口感

conspicuous	*adj.* 明显的
placement	*n.* 放置，布置
aroma	*n.* 气味,风味
seasoning	*n.* 调味品
overriding	*adj.* 最重要的
combat	*v.* 抗击
redress	*v.* 重新调整
dualism	*n.* 两重性，二元论
perpetual	*adj.* 永久的
complement	*v.* 补充
parallel	*adj.* 相似的，对等的
Text 2	
documentary	*n.* 纪录片,文献片
artistry	*n.* 艺术效果,艺术性
blogosphere	*n.* 博客圈
earthy	*adj.* 朴实的
elite	*n.* 精英
mellow	*adj.* 醇香的
feature	*vt.* 以……为特色
pivotal	*adj.* 关键的
dimension	*n.* 尺寸，维度
layout	*n.* 安排，布局
pungent	*adj.* 辛辣的
Text 3	
specialty	*n.* 特产
crispy	*adj.* 脆的
inviting	*adj.* 诱人的；吸引人的
pancake	*n.* 薄饼
splash	*n.* 添加进去的少量
scallion	*n.* 大葱
dress	*v.* 去毛
scald	*v.* 烫洗
oyster	*n.* 牡蛎，蚝

续表

Text 4	
time-honored	*adj.* 历史悠久的
Mung Bean Milk	*n.* 豆汁
tinge	*n.* 少许
Sticky Rice Balls	*n.* 艾窝窝
fillings	*n.* 馅
flexible	*adj.* 柔软的，有弹性的
consistency	*n.* 稠度；平滑度
dainty	*n.* 适口的，味美的
Pea Flour Cake	*n.* 豌豆黄
viscus	*n.* 内脏
tharm	*n.* 肠
Longfusi	*n.* 隆福寺
Huguosi	*n.* 护国寺
temple fair	*n.* 庙会
vendor	*n.* 小贩

Key to Exercises

Exercises 1

Task 1 Short Answer Questions

1. This is because when a single item is cooked on its own, it lacks contrast and therefore lacks harmony.

2. The *yin-yang* principle, i.e. the harmonious balance and contrast in the conspicuous placement of different colors, aroma, flavors, shapes and textures, achieved by varying the ingredients, seasonings, cutting techniques, and cooking methods.

3. The dualism of the Western world argues that good and evil are in perpetual conflict, while *yin-yang* principle believes that *yin* and *yang* complement each other and form a harmonious pair.

4. The Naturalist school of thought holds that nature is made up of varying combinations of five elements of nature: metal, wood, water, fire and earth.

5. China has a wide variety of cuisines in different regions, among which the most influential, representative and socially acknowledged are Lu, Chuan, Yue, Min, Su, Zhe, Xiang and Hui cuisines, often noted as the "Eight Major Cuisines."

Task 2 Reading Comprehension

Part A
1. originate   2. classify   3. concerned   4. harmonious   5. characteristic

Part B
1. C   2. D   3. F   4. A   5. E

Task 3 Translation

A Chinese dish is usually made up of more than one ingredient, because when a single item is cooked on its own, it lacks contrast and therefore lacks harmony. The harmonious balance and contrast of different colors, aroma, flavors, shapes and textures are achieved by varying the ingredients, cutting techniques, seasonings and cooking methods. Yin-yang principle governs all aspects of Chinese people's lives and it has also been the guiding principle for Chinese cooks. All foods are also medicines, the kind of food one eats is closely relevant to one's health. When the yin-yang forces in the body are not balanced, illness results. Now more and more Chinese people have recognized the link between nutrition and health.

Task 4 Omitted

Exercises 2

Task 1 Listening Comprehension
1. B   2. C   3. C   4. A   5. D

Task 2 Spot Dictation

1. producing 2. resident 3. traditional 4. probably 5. easier
6. delicacy 7. shaped 8. In ancient times 9. bringing an end 10. managed to

Task 3 Short Answer Questions

1. A steady temperature must be maintained in the oven and ducks must be rotated so that they are evenly roasted.

2. Mao-tai is a real Chinese specialty. It's strong but won't get into your head.

3. There are approximately more than 200 Beijing snacks and they fall into three varieties: Han, Hui and court snacks.

4. It is said that it came to be called Ai Wo Wo (emperor's special) because one particular emperor loved it so much.

5. Most Beijing snacks can be found around Qianmen Gate, but many Beijingers prefer to go to Longfusi or Huguosi Snack Streets to satisfy their snacking needs.

Task 4 Translation

Beijing has a time-honored history of producing various kinds of snacks. With strong local flavors, Beijing's snacks attract almost all visitors. Mung Bean Milk is one of the most famous Beijing snacks. It tastes mostly sour with a flavor of sweetness, and has a peculiar odor. Because of its low price, it is welcomed by the majority of Beijingers. Another famous snack, Sticky Rice Balls, is a court snack. As white as snow, this delicacy is made of sticky rice. The rice is first steamed then pounded and shaped into a ball. This delicious snack became a favorite of imperial and noble families during the Ming Dynasty; it is said that Ai Wo Wo was once emperor's special.

Unit 7 Chinese Medicine

> **导 读**
> 本单元旨在通过对传统及当代中医及相关知识的介绍，使学生能够运用所学中国文化知识及相关的英语表达进行跨文化交流，弘扬中华医药文化。

Before You Start

While you are preparing for this unit, think about the following questions:

1. How much do you know about traditional Chinese medicine, acupuncture, and famous Chinese medical company Tongrentang (同仁堂)?
2. What do you know about Chinese qi-gong therapy? If there is a foreign friend visiting China, how would you introduce to him/her Chinese physical build-ups?
3. Discuss how people in the western countries treat traditional Chinese medicine, and whether it is meaningful to publicize to western people Chinese medicine as an essential part of Chinese culture.

Section A Reading and Writing

Text 1 An Introduction to Traditional Chinese Medicine

Background

① With a history of 2000 to 3000 years, Traditional Chinese Medicine (TCM) is most influentially originated in the ancient philosophy of Taoism whose main focus is on the observable and natural laws of the universe and the implications for the relationship of human beings to the universe. This long history allows much time for observation, study and speculation by many Taoists. Traditional Chinese medicine yielded a diversity of principles. Below are five of Taoist fundamental principles and applications to health and healing.

- THERE ARE NATURAL LAWS THAT GOVERN THE UNIVERSE.

We are part of the universe and subject to those laws.

- THE NATURAL ORDER OF THE UNIVERSE IS HARMONIOUS AND ORGANIZED.

If we live according to its laws we will be harmonious.

- THE UNIVERSE IS DYNAMIC; CHANGE IS A CONSTANT.

Lack of change disobeys the universe and therefore causes illness.

- ALL LIFE IS INTERCONNECTED AND SYSTEMATICAL.

- HUMANS ARE PART OF THE UNIVERSE. WE ARE INTIMATELY CONNECTED TO THE ENVIRONMENT AND THE UNIVERSE.

Our health is affected by our environment.

② These principles are the axioms about existence that form the foundation for concepts of Yin-Yang, the Five Elements, and Qi. They are also the primary engines of Traditional Chinese Medicine which has evolved and formed a unique system to diagnose and cure illness.

Theoretical Framework of TCM

③ The theories such as Yin-Yang, Qi, and the Five Elements apply the phenomena and laws of nature to study the physiological activities and pathological changes of the human body and its interrelationships.

➢ **Yin-Yang Theory**, the concept of two opposing, yet complementary forces that shape the world and all life, is central to TCM. Yin is cool, night, passive, inward and restful while Yang is hot, day, outward and energetic.

➢ **Qi**, a vital energy or life force, circulates in the body through a system of pathways called meridians. Health is an ongoing process of maintaining balance and harmony in the circulation of Qi.

➢ **The Five Elements**—fire, earth, metal, water, and wood—also utilized by TCM to explain how the body works, for these elements correspond to particular organs and tissues in the body.

All these concepts are documented in *Huang Di Nei Jing* (*Inner Canon of the Yellow Emperor*), one of the classic Chinese medicine texts.

TCM Treatment

TCM emphasizes individualized treatment. Practitioners traditionally use four methods to evaluate a patient's condition: observing (especially the tongue), hearing/smelling, asking/interviewing, and touching/palpating (especially the pulse). They also use a variety of therapies in an effort to promote health and treat diseases. The typical TCM therapies include acupuncture, herbal medicine, qi-gong exercises, moxibustion, cupping, etc.

➢ **Acupuncture.** This treatment is accomplished by stimulating certain areas of the external

body. Practitioners seek to remove blockages in the flow of Qi by stimulating specific points on the body, most often by inserting thin metal needles through the skin.

➢ **Chinese Herbal Medicine.** *The Chinese materia medica* contains hundreds of medicinal substances—primarily plants, but also some minerals and animal products—classified by their perceived action in the body. Different parts of plants such as the leaves, roots, stems, flowers, and seeds are used. Usually, herbs are combined in formulas and given as teas, capsules or powders.

➢ **Qi-gong.** This therapy tries to restore the orderly information flow inside the network through the regulation of Qi.

➢ ④ **Moxibustion.** It's through burning moxa—a cone or stick of dried herb, usually mugwort—on or near the skin, sometimes in conjunction with acupuncture.

➢ **Cupping.** It's to create a slight suction by applying a heated cup to the skin.

Although these therapies appear very different in approach, they all share the same underlying sets of assumptions and insights in the nature of the human body and its place in the universe. Some scientists describe the treatment of diseases through herbal medication, acupuncture, and qi-gong as an "information therapy." (666 words)

Difficult Sentences

① With a history of 2000 to 3000 years, Traditional Chinese Medicine (TCM) is most influentially originated in the ancient philosophy of Taoism whose main focus is on the observable and natural laws of the universe and the implications for the relationship of human beings to the universe.
传统中医历史悠久，长达两三千年，起源于古代道家的哲学思想。道家主要关注宇宙的自然法则和肉眼所能觉察到的现象，及人类与宇宙间的内在关系，这些极大地影响了传统中医。

② These principles are the axioms about existence that form the foundation for concepts of Yin-Yang, the Five Elements, and Qi. They are also the primary engines of Traditional Chinese Medicine which has evolved and formed a unique system to diagnose and cure illness.
这些信念是生存法则，为阴阳学说、五行说、气学说奠定了基础。传统中医吸取这些主要学说，逐渐形成了一套属于自己的诊断治疗疾病的独特理论体系。

③ The theories such as Yin-Yang, Qi, and the Five Elements apply the phenomena and laws of nature to study the physiological activities and pathological changes of the human body and its interrelationships.
阴阳学说、气学说、五行说等运用自然现象和自然法则来研究人类的生理活动、人体内部的病变以及二者之间的关系。

④ Moxibustion. It's through burning moxa—a cone or stick of dried herb, usually mugwort—on or near the skin, sometimes in conjunction with acupuncture.

艾灸是传统中医的一种疗法。把燃烧的艾炷或艾条放在皮肤上或靠近皮肤处以达到治疗目的，有时艾灸和针灸同时施疗。

Text 2 An Introduction to Acupuncture

Acupuncture and moxibustion are the TCM therapies. Their practices are based on meridian theory. According to this theory, Qi and blood circulate in the body through a system of channels called meridians, connecting internal organs with external organs or tissues. ① The flow of Qi and blood can be regulated and diseases are thus treated, by stimulating certain points of the body surface reached by meridians through needling or moxibustion. These stimulation points are called acupuncture points, or acupoints.

Acupoints lie along over a dozen of major meridians. ② There are 12 pairs of regular meridians that are systematically distributed over both sides of the body, and two major extra meridians running along the midlines of the abdomen and back. Along these meridians more than three hundred acupoints are identified, each having its own therapeutic action. For example, the point Hegu, located between the first and second metacarpal bones, can reduce pain in the head and mouth. The point Shenmen, located on the medial end of the transverse crease of the wrist, can induce tranquilization.

In acupuncture clinics, the practitioner first selects appropriate acupoints along different meridians based on identified health problems. Then very fine and thin needles are put into these acupoints. The needles are made of stainless steel and vary in length from half an inch to 3 inches. The choice of needle is usually determined by the location of the acupoint and the effects being sought. ③ If the point is correctly located and the required depth reached, the patient will usually experience a feeling of soreness, heaviness, numbness and distention. The manipulator will simultaneously feel that the needle is tightened.

The needles are usually left at the points for 15–30 minutes. During this time the needles may be manipulated to achieve the effect of tonifying the Qi. ④ Needle manipulations generally include lifting, thrusting, twisting and rotating, based on treatment specifications for the health problem. Needling may also be activated by electrical stimulation, a procedure usually called electro-acupuncture, in which manipulations are achieved through varying frequencies and voltages.

Treatment protocols, frequency and duration are a matter of professional judgment of the practitioner, in consultation with the patient. A common course of treatment may involve between ten and fifteen treatments. In the beginning, it's spaced at about weekly intervals, and spread out to monthly later in a program.

A professional practitioner will always warn the patient of the possibility of worsening the problems or diseases at the start of a course of treatment. The patients may find that in the short term after treatment, the symptoms may in fact get worse before an improvement shows. This is a quite common feature of acupuncture treatment.

The effectiveness of an acupuncture treatment strongly depends on an accurate Chinese medical diagnosis. The needling skills and techniques of the practitioner will also greatly affect the effectiveness of the outcome. Acupuncture can be notably effective in many conditions, but in the West, patients often use acupuncture as the last option for their long-term chronic problems. Therefore, sometimes we regard the treatment as slow and in some cases of marginal benefit. ⑤ With the gradual establishment of acupuncture as the treatment of choice for many people, the effectiveness of the approach to acute or more chronic conditions is being recognized. (552 words)

Difficult Sentences

① The flow of Qi and blood can be regulated and diseases are thus treated, by stimulating certain points of the body surface reached by meridians through needling or moxibustion.
通过针灸或艾灸刺激经络上的穴位，能使气血流通顺畅，治愈疾病。

② There are 12 pairs of regular meridians that are systematically distributed over both sides of the body, and two major extra meridians running along the midlines of the abdomen and back.
常见的12对经络腧穴有规律地分布在身体两侧，此外还有两条经络腧穴位于前胸和后背的中轴线上。

③ If the point is correctly located and the required depth reached, the patient will usually experience a feeling of soreness, heaviness, numbness and distention.
倘若穴位找对了，并且针刺深度也达到要求，患者通常会感觉酸、重、麻和胀。

④ Needle manipulations generally include lifting, thrusting, twisting and rotating, based on treatment specifications for the health problem.
针灸施针通常包括提插与捻转，对症下针。

⑤ With the gradual establishment of acupuncture as the treatment of choice for many people, the effectiveness of the approach to acute or more chronic conditions is being recognized.
随着针灸越来越受人们喜爱，其治疗急病或慢性病的效果也逐渐得到了认可。

Unit 9 Chinese Medicine

Exercises 1

Task 1 Short Answer Questions

Directions: *Read Text 1 and Text 2 first and then answer the following questions briefly.*

1. What does the universe look like according to Taoist laws and principles?

2. What are TCM therapies?

3. What have fostered the formation of a unique system to diagnose and cure illness for TCM?

4. How many pairs of major meridians are distributed over our body?

5. Which of the following is the right picture showing point Hegu?

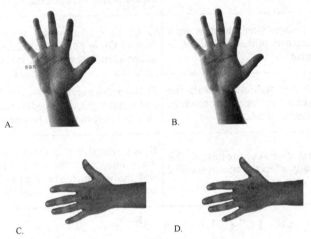

A.   B.

C.   D.

Task 2 Reading Comprehension

Part A

Directions: *In this section, there are 5 incomplete sentences. You are required to select one word for each blank from a list of choices given in the word bank below. You may not use any of the words in the bank more than once.*

chronic	rotate	in consultation with	activate	induce
disobey	simultaneously	in conjunction with	origin	complement

1. During the war, guns and cannons were fired _____.

2. If you find it difficult to solve this abstract mathematic question, the best person I think you can go _____ is Professor Joanna Edwards.

3. Consuming too much meat and too little vegetable usually _____ the unbalance of Ying and Yang.

4. He is suffering from _____ bronchitis.

5. It is universally acknowledged that the moon _____ around the earth.

145

Part B

Directions: *Match the sentences in Column A with the corresponding interpretations in Column B.*

Column A	Column B
1. Practitioners seek to remove blockages in the flow of Qi by stimulating specific points on the body, most often by inserting thin metal needles through the skin.	A. At the beginning of the treatment, patients will usually be reminded of the possible side effects by practitioners.
2. This therapy tries to restore the orderly information flow inside the network through the regulation of Qi.	B. The effectuality of an acupuncture treatment will be largely influenced as well by the needling ways and capabilities of the practitioner.
3. Treatment protocols, frequency and duration are a matter of professional judgment of the practitioner, in consultation with the patient.	C. Qi-gong as a therapy works to manipulate the flow of Qi, in pursuit of making back to normal the information flow within the system.
4. A professional practitioner will always warn the patient of the possibility of worsening the problems or diseases at the start of a course of treatment.	D. If practitioners stimulate certain points on the body, and usually put thin needles made of metal into the skin, the flow of Qi will be smoothened.
5. The needling skills and techniques of the practitioner will also greatly affect the effectiveness of the outcome.	E. An effective therapeutic schedule will not be determined until the practitioner exchanges views with the patient on how often and long the treatment is conducted.

Answers: 1-(   ) 2-(   ) 3-(   ) 4-(   ) 5-(   )

Task 3 Translation

Directions: *Translate the following passage from Chinese into English.*

根据中医理论，气（生命力）、血通过经络腧穴流动全身，连接体内器官和体外器官与组织。针灸诊疗室里，医生根据确诊的症状，顺着不同的经络首先找到正确的穴位。针灸治疗的效果极大地依赖于中医诊断的精确性。

Task 4 Writing

Issue Topic: As we know, herbal medicine, together with acupuncture, is a major pillar of traditional Chinese medicine. However, as the western medical practice is proved to be by nature scientific, many Chinese patients who are sick or get heavy diseases usually resort to doctors of western medicine, for the herbal medicine and acupuncture in traditional medical practice are thought to be unscientifically based, comparatively ineffective and obsolete. Thus, some recommend that the practice of herbal medicine and acupuncture should not be manipulated in the hospitals.

Directions: Write a 200-word response in which you discuss the extent to which you agree or disagree with the recommendation and explain your reasoning for the position you take. In developing and supporting your position, describe specific circumstances in which adopting the recommendation would or would not be advantageous and explain how these examples shape your position.

 VS

Section B Listening and Speaking

Text 3 Situational Dialogue: About Qi-gong Therapy

(P: Peter Cooper, an American graduate student learning Chinese culture in Beijing;
W: Wang Ming, a Chinese graduate student majoring in Chinese medicine.)

W: Hi, Peter. I haven't seen you exercising for quite a long time and you look a bit under the weather. What's wrong?

P: Hi, Wang Ming. Long time no see! During the past two weeks I've got a terrible cold. I feel much better now, but still not in a clear mind.

W: I'm sorry to hear that. But would you mind if I made a suggestion?

P: No. Of course not. We're best friends. Go ahead.

W: Alright. Why not go for a qi-gong therapy. It is an exercise to regulate the mind and breathing in order to control or promote the flow of Qi. If the flow of Qi in your body circulates smoothly, you will regain your clear mind.

P: Wait. Wait. Could you tell me in detail of what Qi is, as it is totally strange and new to me?

W: My pleasure. Just like the theory of yin-yang, Qi is derived from ancient Chinese philosophy, which believes everything is interrelated. In traditional Chinese medicine, Qi is treated as the essential substance of the human body, and its movements explain various life processes. Besides, in its physiological sense, Qi, also known as vital energy, constitutes, supplies and nourishes the human body.

P: I see. But how is Qi related to qi-gong? How do they work together?

W: That's a good question. Qi-gong is an exercise to regulate the mind and breathing in order to control or promote the flow of Qi. Since Qi plays such an important role in the vital processes of the human body, the regulation of Qi flow is therefore used to preserve health and treat disease.

P: That sounds amazing to me. By the way, does qi-gong exercise have something in common with general physical exercise?

W: Actually, they are quite different. Medical qi-gong is practiced to prevent and treat disease and focused on the mobilization of functional potentialities by regulating the mind. But physical exercise is to build up health or restore physical functioning by enhancing strength. What's more, physical exercise uses up energy by tensing muscles and accelerating heart beat and respirations, while qi-gong works to ease, smooth and regulate breathing to store up or accumulate energy in the body.

P: How fantastic it is! I would like to learn qi-gong as a therapy to my health problem. Could you teach me how to practice qi-gong later in the week? Say, Friday, Saturday?

W: No problem. I think I'm free on Friday.

P: Bravo. I can't wait for that moment. See you at 7 am.

W: Ok. See you. (458 words)

Text 4 A Lecture on Beijing Tongrentang

Last time we've talked about the origin and importance of Traditional Chinese Medicine. I think you all have a general idea of that. Right? And for today's Chinese culture class, we're going to talk about Tongrentang, for its significant position in the history of Chinese medicine.

Beijing Tongrentang, founded in 1669, has a history of over 340 years. ① Since the first year of the reign of Emperor Yongzheng in Qing Dynasty, Tongrentang has supplied medicines to the imperial families, serving eight emperors in the 188 years. Wow! That's amazing! Why was

it so favored to emperors? Because the staff of Tongrentang stuck to the inherited motto of "Regardless of how difficult it is to get quality medical materials, no matter how complicated it is to produce medicine, neither funds nor strenuous work is spared." Meanwhile, they also developed a strong sense of self-discipline. No wonder using the best materials and unique traditional prescriptions, the company has produced high-quality Traditional Chinese Medicine (TCM).

② Today, Tongrentang has blended the traditional techniques with modern science and technology, developing into a fairly large modern TCM pharmaceutical (制药的) enterprise group that produces more than 800 products of 24 types of formulation and owns two listed companies and more than 500 drug stores at home and abroad.

As its overall strength is building up, Beijing Tongrentang is also speeding up its international operation. In the four consecutive years since 2002, the company has ranked first in foreign exchange earning among China's TCM companies. Its products are being sold to and well-received in more than 40 countries and regions. ③ With the increase of exports and the growing demand for Tongrentang's products, the company established more than 10 joint ventures, solely invested companies and 20 pharmacies in regions and countries such as the UK, Australia, Thailand, Malaysia, Indonesia, Canada, the United States and South Korea. The pharmacies overseas have inherited the good traditions of Tongrentang. By offering clinical service and retailing medicines, they stress both product sales and cultural communication. With diversified services and products, Tongrentang pharmacies are offering quality and efficient services to overseas patients and consumers, achieving remarkable business and social benefits.

To quicken the step of internationalization, Beijing Tongrentang TCM Co., Ltd. was set up in Hong Kong. It would develop more TCM and health products by making full use of the advantages in Hong Kong, adopting international standards in techniques, manufacturing and marketing.

To sum up, over three hundred years of history fills the staff of Tongrentang with pride. ④ Successful listings in Shanghai and Hong Kong, bold experiment with e-commerce and rapid establishment of hundreds of branches at home and abroad, steady implementation of strategy of building a health industry group have also revitalized the ancient but modern enterprise. Looking into the future, Beijing Tongrentang should spare no effort in combining the gist of traditional medicine with modern technology to make its due contributions to the rejuvenation of the TCM industry.

That's all for today's Chinese culture class. Please go over it after class and prepare for the quiz about Tongrentang next class. (522 words)

Difficult Sentences

① Since the first year of the reign of Emperor Yongzheng in Qing Dynasty, Tongrentang has supplied medicines to the imperial families, serving eight emperors in the 188 years.
自清朝雍正元年开始，同仁堂正式供奉清皇宫御药房用药，历经八代皇帝，长达188年。

② Today, Tongrentang has blended the traditional techniques with modern science and technology, developing into a fairly large modern TCM pharmaceutical enterprise group that produces more than 800 products of 24 types of formulation and owns two listed companies and more than 500 drug stores at home and abroad.
现在，同仁堂秉承传统工艺并结合现代科技，成为一家大型的现代传统中药企业集团，生产24个剂型、800余种产品，此外还拥有两家上市公司以及分布在国内外的500多家药店。

③ With the increase of exports and the growing demand for Tongrentang's products, the company established more than 10 joint ventures, solely invested companies and 20 pharmacies in regions and countries such as the UK, Australia, Thailand, Malaysia, Indonesia, Canada, the United States and South Korea.
随着产品出口和需求增加，北京同仁堂成立了10余家合资公司、独资公司以及20

家药店，遍布英国、澳大利亚、泰国、马来西亚、印度尼西亚、加拿大、美国、韩国等国家和地区。

④ Successful listings in Shanghai and Hong Kong, bold experiment with e-commerce and rapid establishment of hundreds of branches at home and abroad, steady implementation of strategy of building a health industry group have also revitalized the ancient but modern enterprise.

通过在上海、香港成功上市，大胆开拓电子商务，迅速建起国内外几百家分店以及组建健康药业集团策略的实施，北京同仁堂焕发新生，已成为一个融汇古今的企业。

Exercises 2

Task 1 Listening Comprehension

Directions: *Listen to the Situational Dialogue in Text 3, read the four choices marked A, B, C and D, and decide which is the best answer.*

1. Where does the conversation take place?
    A. In the school playground.　　B. In the clinic.
    C. In the hospital.　　D. In the qi-gong Class.
2. What's wrong with Peter?
    A. He has got a fever in the past two weeks.
    B. He doesn't feel very well because his mind has been injured in the past two weeks.
    C. He doesn't feel himself because he has got a cold in the past two weeks.
    D. He lost his mind because of a terrible cold in the past two weeks.
3. Based on Wang Ming's introduction, which of the following is NOT right about Qi?
    A. It is derived from ancient Chinese Confucian philosophy and known as "vital energy."
    B. It is regarded as the fundamental substance of the human body.
    C. It is related to various life processes, constituting, replenishing and nourishing human body.
    D. The regulation of Qi flow is used to preserve health and treat disease.
4. How is qi-gong exercise related to Qi?
    A. Qi comes from qi-gong exercise, as qi-gong controls and promotes the flow of Qi.
    B. qi-gong exercise helps regulate the mind and breathing to control or promote the flow of Qi.
    C. qi-gong exercise produces Qi to regulate the mind and breathing.
    D. Qi helps qi-gong exercise, as the flow of Qi can regulate the mind and breathing.
5. Which of the following is right of general physical exercise?
    A. It is only to enhance strength.
    B. It is almost the same as medical qi-gong exercise.
    C. It is to build up health or restore physical functioning.
    D. It is generally believed not as good as qi-gong.

Unit 9 Chinese Medicine

Task 2 Spot Dictation

Directions: *In this section you will hear the passage based on Text 4 three times. When the passage is read for the first time, you should listen carefully for its general idea. When the passage is read for the second time, you are required to fill in the blanks with the exact words you have just heard. Finally, when the passage is read for the third time, you should check what you have written.*

Today's lecture is on the status of Beijing Tongrentang in the history of Chinese medicine. Beijing Tongrentang was established in 1669, with a long history of more than (1)_____ years. Providing medicines to the imperial families, it has served eight emperors for (2)_____ years. Traditionally it has strictly followed the (3)_____ motto, developing a strong sense of (4)_____ and producing high-quality Traditional Chinese Medicine by using the best materials and unique traditional (5)_____. Nowadays it gradually develops into a fairly large modern TCM pharmaceutical enterprise. With its comprehensive power (6)_____, it has also established many joint ventures, (7)_____ companies and pharmacies overseas. Although a larger and international company, it stresses much on tradition, offering quality and efficient clinical service and (8)_____ diversified medicines to patients and consumers. Beijing Tongrentang TCM Co., Ltd in Hong Kong has been set up, combining the (9)_____ of traditional medicine with modern science and technology. It is now highly expected to make great (10)_____ to the TCM industry.

Task 3 Short Answer Questions

Directions: *Read Text 4 and answer the following questions briefly.*

1. What is the last lecture mainly about?
2. In which dynasty was Beijing Tongrentang founded?
3. How many countries and regions are the products being sold to and well-received in?
4. What is our great expectation of Beijing Tongrentang in the future?

Task 4 Translation

Directions: *Translate the following passage from Chinese into English.*

在300多年的风雨历程中，历代同仁堂人始终恪守"炮制虽繁必不敢省人工，品味虽贵必不敢减物力"的古训。北京同仁堂的产品以其"配方独特、选料上乘、工艺精湛、疗效显著"而享誉海内外。随着综合实力的提高，北京同仁堂也加快其国际业务。

Words and Expressions for Chinese Medicine

Text 1	
axiom	*n.* 原理
pathological	*adj.* 病理的
meridians	*n.* 经络腧穴
moxibustion	*n.* 艾灸

materia medica	药物学
mugwort	n. 艾蒿
implication	n. 涵义，暗指
speculation	n. 推测，思考
fundamental	adj. 基本的，根本的
harmonious	adj. 协调的，和睦的
systematical	adj. 有系统的
intimately	adv. 紧密地，亲密地
diagnose	v. 诊断，判断
circulate	v. 使循环，使流通
practitioner	n. 实践者，行医者
formula	n. 公式，准则，配方
capsule	n. 胶囊
therapy	n. 治疗，疗法
in conjunction with	共同，与……协力
assumption	n. 假定，猜想
Text 2	
acupoint	n. 穴位
Hegu	n. 合谷穴
metacarpal	adj. 掌部的
Shenmen	n. 神门穴
tranquilization	n. 使安静（安神）
distention	n. 膨胀，扩张
manipulator	n. 施针者
tonifying	adj. 滋补的
Treatment protocol	治疗方案
simultaneously	adv. 同时发生地
Text 4	
be favored to	受宠于……
stick to the inherited motto	恪守古训
develop a strong sense of self-discipline	树立强烈的自律意识
strenuous	adj. 艰苦的，费力的
traditional prescription	传统处方
blend	v. 混合，融合

续表

pharmaceutical enterprise group	医药企业集团
type of formulation	剂型
listed company	上市公司
drug store	药店
consecutive	*adj.* 连续的,连贯的
foreign exchange	外汇
well-received	*adj.* 受欢迎的
joint venture	合资企业
solely invested company	独资企业
pharmacy	*n.* 药房
clinical service	门诊服务,诊疗服务
retail	*v.* 零售
diversified	*adj.* 多样化的
remarkable	*adj.* 卓越的,非凡的
franchise operation	特许经营
chain store	连锁店
implement	*v.* 实施,执行,实现

Key to Exercises

Exercises 1

Task 1 Short Answer Questions
1. The universe is dynamic, constantly changeable, and systematical.
2. They include acupuncture, herbal medicine, qi-gong exercises, moxibustion, cupping etc.
3. Yin-Yang, the Five Elements, and Qi.
4. 12 pairs
5. D

Task 2 Reading Comprehension
Part A
1. simultaneously   2. in consultation with   3. induces   4. chronic   5. rotates

Part B
1. D   2. C   3. E   4. A   5. B

Task 3 Translation
According to the theory of Traditional Chinese Medicine, Qi (vital energy or life force) and blood circulate in the body through a system of channels called meridians, connecting internal organs with external organs or tissues. In an acupuncture clinic, the practitioner first selects appropriate acupoints along different meridians based on identified health problems. The effectiveness of an acupuncture treatment is strongly dependent upon an accurate Chinese medical diagnosis.

Task 4 Writing
Sample Writing
Traditional Chinese medicine is most famous for its herbal medicine and acupuncture, but its treatment is challenged and even thought to be devoid of scientific support by some people. The statement hastily and unreasonably recommends that the practices of herbal medicine and acupuncture should not be manipulated in hospital and makes an unfair neglect of the advantages of traditional Chinese medicine practice.

It is acknowledged that the western medical practice is supported by scientific experiments and proves effective in treatment. The traditional Chinese medicine displaying its far-reaching significant effects on medicine history actually proves to be the first step in human's discovery on medicine practice, much earlier than the western medicine.

The western medicine and the traditional Chinese medicine inevitably demonstrate their own weaknesses, apart from strengths. The doctors of western medicine like to use antibiotics to fight against the bacteria. However, the abuse of antibiotics will decrease resistance created by human's own body. Compared with western medicine, traditional Chinese medicine takes much longer time for patients to recover, and the herbal medicines taste more terrible. What's more, acupuncture seems to foreigners a little bit hazardous and unscientific, and thus few people will be brave enough to try it.

With the development of science, the effectiveness of traditional Chinese medicine will surely be proved and contribute much in treatment like western medicine. The combination of both may achieve better treatment results. Since the most important thing of medicine whether western or traditional Chinese is to preserve the health of human beings, any useful treatment should be manipulated in hospital. (259 words)

Exercises 2

Task 1 Listening Comprehension
1. A   2. C   3. A   4. B   5. C

Task 2 Spot Dictation
1. 340   2. 188   3. inherited   4. self-discipline   5. prescriptions
6. growing up/building up   7. solely invested   8. retails   9. gist   10. contributions

Task 3 Short Answer Questions
1. It is mainly about the significant origin of Traditional Chinese Medicine.
2. Beijing Tongrentang was founded in 1669, which was in Qing Dynasty.
3. More than 40 countries and regions.
4. Beijing Tongrentang should try its best to combine the gist of traditional medicine with modern technology.

Task 4 Translation
Over the past 300 years, the staff of Tongrentang has stuck to the motto of "Regardless how difficult it is to get quality medical materials, no matter how complicated it is to produce medicine, neither funds nor strenuous work is spared." Using the best materials and unique traditional prescriptions, the company has produced high-quality Traditional Chinese Medicine (TCM) and made Tongrentang well-known home and abroad. As its overall strength is building up, Beijing Tongrentang is also speeding up its international operation business.

Unit 10 National Treasures

> **导 读**
>
> 本单元旨在通过对武术、太极拳、剪纸、刺绣、瓷器、京剧等中华民族传统文化瑰宝的介绍，使学生了解相关文化知识及其英语表达，进而增强跨文化交流能力，以便更好地完成传播中华文化的使命。

Before You Start

While you are preparing for this unit, think about the following questions:

1. Before learning this unit, please consider what you know about Chinese Wushu. Do you ever long for possessing Kung Fu yourself? Tell us your favorite Kung Fu player, if any, in China.
2. What do you know about Tai Ji Quan? What are the correlations between Tai Ji Quan and Taoism?

Section A   Reading and Writing

Text 1 Wushu and Tai Ji Quan

Wushu, or martial arts, is an important component of the cultural heritage of China, with a rich content over the centuries. Literally, "Wu" means military, and "shu" means art. Wushu therefore means the art of fighting, or martial arts. Martial training includes Ti (kicking), Da (punching), Shuai (throwing), Na (controlling), Ji (hitting), Ci (thrusting), etc.

Wushu was born and has steadily grown and attained perfection as an integral part of Chinese culture. As such it is bound to be influenced and conditioned by other forms of culture, first and foremost by philosophy, art and literature, and religion. Wushu reigns as one of the most traditional and popular national sports in China, practiced by the young and old alike.

Wushu was originally a military training method, bearing a

close relationship with ancient combats. Practical skills, such as strength training, fencing, staff sparring, spear training, etc., are still used now by policemen and soldiers. Today Wushu has been organized and systematized into a formal branch of study in the performance arts and has become an athletic and aesthetic performance and competitive sport. Every movement must exhibit sensible combat application and aestheticism.

Chinese Wushu is classified into various styles according to different sects, families and schools, as well as different fighting techniques. Routines are performed solo, paired or in groups, either barehanded or armed with traditional Chinese weaponry. Wushu can be viewed in terms of two categories, including Taolu (set forms) and Gongfang (offence and defense).

Tai Ji Quan is a major division of Chinese martial arts. Tai Ji Quan means "supreme ultimate fist." Tai means "Supreme," Ji means "Ultimate," and Quan means "Fist."

There have been different sayings about the origin of Tai Ji Quan. The traditional legend goes that the wise man Zhang Sanfeng of the Song Dynasty (960—1279) created Tai Ji Quan after he had witnessed a fight between a sparrow and a snake; while most people agreed that the modern Tai Ji Quan originated from Chen style Tai Ji Quan, which first appeared during the 19th century in the Daoguang Reign of the Qing Dynasty (1644—1911).

① Tai Ji Quan has its philosophical roots in Taoism and is considered as an internal martial art, utilizing the internal energy, or Qi, and following the simple principle of "subduing the vigorous by the soft." ② Taoism is the oldest philosophy of China which is represented by the famous symbol of the Yin and Yang that generate the continuous flow of Qi in a circular motion bringing existence to the physical and metaphysical world.

Nowadays Wushu's emphasis has shifted from combat to performance, and it is practiced to remain healthy, attain self-defense skills and mental discipline, and achieve recreational pursuit. In 1990, Wushu was adopted as an official medal event in the Asian Games, and since then World Championships have been held with 56 nations participating. Now Wushu is vying for the Olympic Games in the 21st century. (493 words)

 Difficult Sentences

① Tai Ji Quan has its philosophical roots in Taoism and is considered as an internal martial art, utilizing the internal energy, or Qi, and following the simple principle of "subduing the vigorous by the soft".

太极拳是运用传统道家哲学原理，充分利用身体内在能量，或者气，并秉承"以柔克刚"法则的一种内功。

② Taoism is the oldest philosophy of China which is represented by the famous symbol of the Yin and Yang that generate the continuous flow of Qi in a circular motion bringing existence to the physical and metaphysical world.
道家思想是中国最古老的哲学思想，以阴阳学说为主。阴阳生气，气循环流转，进而生成万物。

Text 2 Chinese Handicrafts

Probably it's true that you can tell a nation by its handicrafts. The handicraft industry at its very beginning marked the civilization. It then kept evolving and finally appears gorgeous today.

When wonderful items break upon you, in your consciousness you may wonder at their past. You may also wonder why they have existed and the role they have played. Probably you like to think that they are living things.

Actually, Chinese handicrafts are created to be living things. It has been the highest level pursued by countless artisans on their works. You may think the norm abstract, intricate, or mysterious, but when you see close to some works, you would feel an undercurrent of power flowing in them. Probably that's what the oriental art suggests to its viewers.

Paper-cut

Paper-cut is a type of cutting art, as well as the most popular folk art in China. The first paper-cut can be traced back to the Northern and Southern Dynasties (386-581) period. The initiation and spread of paper-cuts had a close relationship with Chinese rural festivals. People pasted paper-cuts on walls, windows and doors at wedding ceremonies or festivals to enhance the festive atmosphere.

Chinese paper-cuts are rich in content. The auspicious designs symbolize good luck and the avoidance of evil. The child, lotus and bottle gourd designs suggest a family with a large number of children and grandchildren. Domestic birds, livestock, fruit, fish and worms are also familiar objects depicted by Chinese farmers. Paper-cuts made in different areas have different characteristics. Shaanxi window paper-cuts are simple and bold; paper-cuts from Hebei province and Shanxi province are bright in color; while papercuts in southern provinces are delicate and fine.

Su Embroidery

With a history of more than 3,000 years, Su embroidery is the general name for embroidery products in areas around Suzhou, Jiangsu province. There emerged many embroidery workshops and embroidery markets in the Song Dynasty. Up to Ming and Qing Dynasties its embroidery flourished for a time.

Su embroidery is famous for its elaborateness and elegance. It used to be made by the unmarried daughters of noble families.

① Its characteristics include elegant colors, fine needling, the application of halo dyeing, and the vacant lines left between colors. ② Its pattern themes vary from "the celebration of harvest," "wealthy family," "dragon and phoenix symbolic of the propitious" to "well-being through hundreds of years," "happy encounter," and "abundance in family members." There are many other embroidered products, such as dress and adornments, beddings and ornaments attached to the waist.

Porcelain

Porcelain has been in use for over 4000 years in China. It is made from special white clay and fired at a temperature of 1280 degrees centigrade. There are a couple of different ways in which these items are decorated, the most common today being molding, decorating, and glazing.

故宫宝物之青花瓷瓶

The temperature is usually above 600 degrees centigrade. Any mistake in temperature will cause wrong colors or sheds of glaze which lend to failure. The Chinese have always been extremely proficient at porcelain work, and have produced numerous pieces that look like coral, glass, stone, and many other materials.

Jingtailan

燕京四绝

Jingtailan (Cloisonné) has a history of over 500 years. Its art is a unique combination of sculpture, painting, porcelain making and copper-smithing that is said to have originated in Beijing during the Yuan Dynasty (1271—1368). The oldest extant piece was made during the Yuan Dynasty, but Jingtailan underwent a major change during the Ming Dynasty when a new blue pigment was discovered at about 1450 to 1456, which gave Jingtailan its current name based on the Chinese word "lan" for blue. Nevertheless, Jingtailan reached its peak during the Qing Dynasty (1644—1911) due to great innovations in copper-melting techniques. The making of Jingtailan requires rather elaborate and complicated processes; all the products are elegant in molding, dazzling in colors and graceful in design. It enjoys a high reputation both at home and abroad with most of its products for export. (662 words)

(*Adapted from http://www.estudychinese.com*)

 ## Difficult Sentences

① Its characteristics include elegant colors, fine needling, the application of halo dyeing (晕染), and the vacant lines left between colors.
苏绣色彩清新高雅，织工精巧细腻，常以晕染与空间留白为其特色。

② Its pattern themes vary from "the celebration of harvest," "wealthy family," "dragon and phoenix symbolic of the propitious (吉祥的)" to "well-being through hundreds of years,"

"happy encounter," and "abundance in family members."
刺绣图案内容丰富，如庆祝丰收、丰衣足食、龙凤呈祥、健康长寿、美好邂逅、人丁兴旺等。

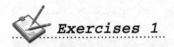 Exercises 1

Task 1 Short Answer Questions

Directions: *Read Text 1 and Text 2 and then answer the following questions briefly.*

1. What does "Wushu" mean literally?
2. What is the philosophical root of Tai Ji Quan?
3. What are the benefits of practicing Wushu?
4. What do auspicious paper-cuts symbolize in content?
5. What is Su embroidery famous for?

Task 2 Reading Comprehension

Part A

Directions: *Complete the following sentences with the proper form of the words given in the brackets.*

1. We have to _____ (system) our filing so it is easier to find correspondence.
2. Many of these problems can be minimized by _____ (sense) planning.
3. He was _____ (philosophy) about losing and said that he'd be back next year to try again.
4. It was Christmas and everyone was in _____ (festival) mood.
5. The dove is _____ (symbol) of peace.

Part B

Directions: *In this section, you are going to read a passage with five statements attached to it. Each statement contains information given in one of the paragraphs. Identify the paragraph from which the information is derived. Each paragraph is marked with a letter.*

   A) Wushu covers a vast array of Chinese martial arts, including those forms of kung fu made famous by movie stars such as Bruce Lee and Jet Li. It has won over many foreign fans thanks to its dynamic moves and distinctive culture. Yet the sport struggles to hold the attention of Chinese students, who show more interest in NBA stars.

   B) To improve grassroots involvement, the General Administration of Wushu has drafted a proposal to introduce martial arts into the physical education curricula of China's primary and secondary schools, while calling for favorable scoring policies in the entrance exam. Popular styles such as changquan, taijiquan (tai chi) and nanquan would be compiled in textbooks and drills would be practiced in PE classes under the guidance of trained teachers. Students who obtain high levels should also be awarded extra points in the entrance exam.

   C) PE activities on campus should be diversified, with more events like Wushu, but the risks of practicing martial arts have led to some concerns. How to make it safe and easy to practice while keeping it appealing is an issue.

D) "If we simplify Wushu into slow-motion, non-contact stunts like radio calisthenics（健美操）to make sure it's safe, it will become boring and students won't buy it," Kang Gewu, secretary-general of the Chinese Martial Arts Research Institute said. "It won't reflect the deep traditional and cultural roots either."

E) Despite doubts, some school leaders have shown interest in cultivating future kung fu stars on campus. "I think it's a good thing to try," said Wang Tao, vice-president of Beijing 101 Middle School. "Look at taekwondo（跆拳道）, how popular it is (with teenagers). Why not let Wushu in? We might discover some students who could be movie stars."

(　) 1. There are some concerns about the safety of the practice of martial arts in schools.
(　) 2. Chinese young people today show mor interest in western sports than in Chinese traditional sports like martial arts.
(　) 3. It is proposed to include Wushu art into PE curricula of Chinese schools.
(　) 4. It is expected that Wushu art on campus may lead to the development of kungfu stars of the future.
(　) 5. Some extra points will be granted in the entrance exam if students obtain good achievement in Wushu art.

Task 3　Translation

Directions: *Translate the following passage from Chinese into English.*

剪纸是中国最流行的传统民间艺术之一。中国的剪纸有一千五百多年的历史，在明朝和清朝时期特别流行。剪纸的产生和传播与中国农村的节日有密切关系。婚礼或节日里人们在墙、窗户和门上贴剪纸以增加喜庆气氛。剪纸常用的颜色是红色，象征健康和兴旺。

Task 4　Writing

Directions: *Learn something about Taoism and write a research report on the relationship between Taoism and Tai Ji Quan.*

Section B　Listening and Speaking

Text 3　Situational Dialogue: Beijing Opera

(*A: Susan; B: Lin Xiao*)

A: I went to see Beijing Opera last night. It's fantastic!
B: Great. What repertoire did you see?
A: Umm— ① Beats me. I don't remember the name. But the story is about a defeated king whose concubine killed herself.

霸王别姬

B: That must be "The King Says Farewell to His Concubine"[1]
A: That's it! It's really a moving story.
B: It is amazing that you can understand Beijing Opera.
A: Thanks. Actually, there are English lines shown beside the stage.
B: So what do you think of Beijing Opera?
A: Well, it is an admirable art and at the same time a difficult abstract art.
B: So it is. ② Beijing Opera synthesizes music, drama, dancing, and acrobatics along with very elaborate costumes and a minimum of props, according to traditions and customs dating back as far as the twelfth century.
A: Oh, I don't know that! But I enjoy the costumes and facial masks better. They are more attractive.
B: Absolutely. There is very distinct Ming Dynasty influence on Beijing Opera costumes. They are colorful and majestic.
A: Yes. The two long pieces of white silk at the end of the sleeves create a graceful feeling during dancing. It seems that different styles of costumes are used to reflect the status of different characters, right?
B: Wow you can see that? It's really awesome! Definitely there are more decorations in the costumes of the nobles, while those of the poor tend to be simple and less ornamental.
A: But why are there so many colors for facial masks? Do they have special meanings?
B: Yes. Facial masks use different colors as important ways to portray a character. There are hundreds of different facial mask designs and each character has its own design. For example, Guan Yu is a very well-known warrior. People believe he had a dark-red complexion. So his facial mask is painted red, because red is a color to represent loyalty and courage.
A: So colors become an important expression.
B: Yes, people can tell a hero from a villain by the colors of the masks. ③ In general, white usually represents treachery; black represents righteousness; yellow represents bravery; blue and green represent rebellious fighters; while gold and silver represent divinity and Buddhism.
A: I didn't realize Beijing Opera facial mask is so complicated. You guys are lucky to have such wonderful heritage.
B: Yes, we are. But Beijing Opera has problems in appealing to the young people and there are not many fans of Beijing Opera left. Many people are worried about its future.
A: Yeah, that's too bad. Maybe because it's too slow and monotonous. Anyway, that is a common problem for all classic arts. But I believe there will always be some people who like it and pass it on to the next generation.

1　《霸王别姬》是京剧艺术大师梅兰芳表演的梅派经典名剧之一。

Unit 10 *National Treasures*

B: So do I. Listen, let's go to see a Beijing Opera together some time!
A: That would be great! (499 words)

Difficult Sentences

① beats me 的意思是"把我难倒了，我也不懂"。

② Beijing Opera synthesizes music, drama, dancing, and acrobatics along with very elaborate costumes and a minimum of props(道具), according to traditions and customs dating back as far as the twelfth century.
京剧以12世纪中国传统习俗为依据，融音乐、戏剧、舞蹈、杂技以及精美的服饰与道具为一体。

③ In general, white usually represents treachery; black represents righteousness; yellow represents bravery; blue and green represent rebellious fighters; while gold and silver represent divinity and Buddhism.
总体来说，白脸代表奸诈多疑；黑脸代表正直严肃；黄脸代表勇猛暴躁；蓝脸代表桀骜不驯；金脸和银脸代表神圣和佛性。

Text 4 A Tour Guide Commentary on Dashilar

It takes dozens of steps to walk from southwest of Tian'anmen Square to the east end of Dashilar Street. The overall length of Dashilar is 275 m from east to west. The prosperous classes of the ancient capital nurtured its business and now the old street is famous for all kinds of stores with an antique flavor. Many people come here to experience the relics of historic wealth. The average customer flow reaches 150—160 thousand usually and increases to more than 200 thousand on weekends and in holidays.

Dashilar originated in Yuan Dynasty (1271—1368) and was finally built in Ming Dynasty (1368—1644) by local people, who put wooden fences at both ends of the street. In Qing Dynasty (1644—1911) and beyond, Dashilar was enlarged and grew in prosperity day by day. Since then the hutong acquired its name: Dashilar.

Although this commercial street has a history of more than 580 years, most of the ancient architectures are well preserved and many famous old shops and time-honored brands in old Beijing still provide good products. The time-honored-brand Stores, such as Tongrentang Chinese herbal medicine store, Rui Fu Xiang silk store, Ma Ju Yuan hat store, Nei Lian Sheng shoe store, Zhang Yi Yuan tea shop, and Liu Bi Ju pickle shop, are over 100 years old.

① There once was a widespread saying in Beijing that if you want to watch sideshows, go on the overbridge; if you want to go shopping, Dashilar is the place. ② "Wearing the hats of Ma Ju Yuan, standing in the shoes of Nei Lian Sheng, owning the silk fabric of Rui Fu Xiang and taking the money of Si Da Heng Banks" — these all make you part of the prosperous scene of this commercial street in old Beijing.

Dashilar was also the former entertainment center of Beijing apart from the commercial center. It was the leading birthplace of Beijing opera and Xuannan Culture[1], which constitutes an important factor of the Capital Culture. In history, there were five grand Chinese opera theaters in Dashilar—Qingle Yuan, Sanqing Yuan, Guangde Lou, Guanghe Yuan, Tongle Yuan. The first cinema in Beijing—Daguan Lou building was also situated there. ③ The combination of royal culture and folk culture makes Dashilar a place with profound cultural foundation and dignified historical atmosphere. (392 words)

 Difficult Sentences

① There once was a widespread saying in Beijing that if you want to watch sideshows, go on the overbridge; if you want to go shopping, Dashilar is the place.
老北京有句顺口溜叫"看玩意上天桥，买东西到大栅栏"。

② "Wearing the hats of Ma Ju Yuan, standing in the shoes of Nei Lian Sheng, owning the silk fabric of Rui Fu Xiang and taking the money of Si Da Heng Banks" —these all make you part of the prosperous scene of this commercial street in old Beijing.
"头顶马聚元，脚踩内联升，身穿瑞蚨祥，腰缠四大恒"说的都是早年间大栅栏的地位和繁华景象。

③ The combination of royal culture and folk culture makes Dashilar a place with profound cultural foundation and dignified history atmosphere.
宫廷文化与民俗文化的结合使大栅栏成为一个具有深邃文化底蕴与厚重历史氛围的地方。

---

1 北京的宣南泛指今宣武门外至广安门内外一带，自明清以来，士人文化与平民文化在此蓬勃发展，形成了集通俗、儒雅、华丽于一身的宣南文化，并与皇城文化并肩而立，促成了明、清两代北京的空前繁荣。

Exercises 2

Task 1 Listening Comprehension

Directions: *Listen to the Situational Dialogue in Text 3, read the four choices marked A, B, C and D, and decide which is the best answer.*

1. Beijing Opera reflects traditions and customs dating back as far as _____.
   A. the twelfth century   B. the tenth century
   C. Ming Dynasty   D. Yuan Dynasty
2. What does the color black represent for facial masks?
   A. Treachery.   B. Buddhism.
   C. Rebelliousness.   D. Righteousness.
3. What does the color yellow represent for facial masks?
   A. Loyalty.   B. Courage.
   C. Bravery.   D. Divinity.
4. What does the color red represent for facial masks?
   A. Loyalty.   B. Treachery.
   C. Rebelliousness.   D. Divinity.
5. What color does the character of Guanyu wear?
   A. Dark-red.   B. Gold.
   C. Blue and green.   D. Yellow.

Task 2 Spot Dictation

Directions: *In this section you will hear the passage based on Text 4 three times. When the passage is read for the first time, you should listen carefully for its general idea. When the passage is read for the second time, you are required to fill in the blanks with the exact words you have just heard. Finally, when the passage is read for the third time, you should check what you have written.*

It takes dozens of steps to walk from southwest of Tian'anmen Square to the east end of Dashilar Street. The prosperous classes of the ancient capital (1)_____ its business and now, the old street is (2)_____ all kinds of stores with an antique (3)_____. Many people come here to experience the (4)_____ of historic wealth.

Dashilar (5)_____ Yuan Dynasty and was finally built in Ming Dynasty by local people, who put wooden fences at both ends of the street. In Qing Dynasty and beyond, Dashilar was enlarged and grew in (6)_____ day by day. Since then the hutong (7)_____ its name: Dashilar.

Although this commercial street has a history of more than 580 years, most of the ancient architectures are well (8)_____ and many famous old shops and time-honored brands in old Beijing still provide good products. Dashilar was also the former entertainment center of Beijing (9)_____ the commercial center. It was the leading birthplace of Beijing opera and Xuannan Culture, which (10)_____ an important factor of the Capital Culture.

Task 3 Short Answer Questions

Directions: *Read Text 3 and Text 4 first, and then answer the following questions briefly.*
1. What forms of art does Beijing Opera synthesize?
2. What influenced Beijing Opera costumes to be colorful and majestic?
3. Why are colors important for facial masks?
4. Why was Dashilar the former commercial center of Beijing?
5. Why was Dashilar the former entertainment center of Beijing?

Task 4 Translation

Directions: *Translate the following passage from Chinese into English.*

大栅栏以古色古香的各种商店而闻名。 每天的平均客流量达到15万到16万人，周末和假期超过20万人。 虽然这条商业街有580多年的历史，但大多数的古代建筑依然保存完好。很多著名的老店和老北京知名品牌仍在提供优质的产品。宫廷文化与民俗文化的结合使大栅栏成为一个具有深邃文化底蕴与厚重历史氛围的地方。

Words and Phrases for National Treasures

Text 1	
martial arts	武术
reign	*v.* 盛行
staff sparring	棍法
aesthetic	*adj.* 美学的
sect	*n.* (武术)派
family	*n.* (武术)家
school	*n.* (武术)门
weaponry	*n.* 武器（总称）
subdue	*v.* 制服
metaphysical	*adj.* 形而上的
vie	*v.* 竞争
Text 2	
handicraft	*n.* 手工艺
auspicious	*adj.* 吉祥的
gourd	*n.* 葫芦
livestock	*n.* 家畜
embroidery	*n.* 刺绣
halo dyeing	*n.* 晕染
propitious	*adj.* 吉祥的
porcelain	*n.* 陶瓷

续表

mold	v. 用模子做，浇铸
glaze	v. 上釉
enamel	v. 上珐琅
copper-smithing	n. 铜作
extant	adj. 现存的
pigment	n. 颜料
calisthenics	n. 健美操
Text 3	
repertoire	n.（全部）剧目
concubine	n. 妾，妃子
prop	n. 道具
facial mask	n. 脸谱
treachery	n. 背叛
righteousness	n. 正义
divinity	n. 神性
monotonous	adj. 单调乏味的
Text 4	
relic	n. 遗迹
sideshow	n. 助兴表演，杂耍

Key to Exercises

Before You Start

1. What do you know about Chinese Wushu? Tell us your favorite Kung Fu player in China.

I may not know Chinese Kung Fu very much but I like it, because it is one of our national treasures. Among Chinese Kung Fu players, my favorite one is Jackie Chan, star of the Kung Fu Movie industry. He has been attracting audiences the world over for more than a decade. His worldwide popularity today, with more than fifty films to his name, is an ongoing phenomenon. He incorporated the idea of Chinese martial arts into his film and even became a martial arts director. By the late seventies, he introduced Kung Fu Comedy and was welcomed by the audience. Today, he continues to make at least one film a year and remains the world's number-one action star, never ceasing to amaze his audience!

2. What can you say about Tai Ji Quan? What are the correlations between Tai Ji Quan and Taoism?

Many people in China are now playing Tai Ji Quan for maintaining healthy body condition. It is like a soft Kung Fu—with Qi circulating in body and getting a balance among various body functions.

Tai Ji Quan has its philosophical roots in Taoism and is considered as an internal martial art, utilizing the internal energy, or Qi, and following the simple principle of "subduing the vigorous by the soft." Taoism is the oldest philosophy of China which is represented by the famous symbol of the Yin and Yang that generate the continuous flow of Qi in a circular motion bringing existence to the physical and metaphysical world.

Exercises 1

Task 1 Short Answer Questions

1. "Wu" means military, and "shu" means art. Wushu therefore means the art of fighting, or martial arts.

2. Tai Ji Quan has its philosophical roots in Taoism and is considered as an internal martial art.

3. It is practiced to remain healthy, attain self-defense skills and mental discipline, and achieve recreational pursuit.

4. The auspicious designs symbolize good luck and the avoidance of evil.

5. Su embroidery is famous for its elaborateness and elegance.

Task 2 Reading Comprehension
Part A

1. systematize   2. sensible   3. philosophical   4. festive   5. symbolic

Part B
1. C   2. A   3. B   4. E   5. B

Task 3 Translation

Paper-cut is one of China's most popular traditional folk arts. Chinese paper-cut has a history of more than 1500 years, and it was widespread particularly during the Ming and Qing Dynasties. The initiation and spread of paper-cuts has a close relationship with Chinese rural festivals. People paste paper-cuts on walls, windows and doors at wedding ceremonies or festivals to enhance joyful atmosphere. The color frequently used in paper-cuts is red, which symbolizes health and prosperity.

Task 4 Writing
Sample Writing

Many people have heard about Tai Ji, and they believe that Tai Ji means Tai Ji Quan, which is one kind of ancient Chinese Martial Arts. However, Tai Ji is also an essential concept of Taoism. Tai Ji gives birth to two poles: one is Yang Pole, and the other Yin Pole. If you failed to understand the concept of Yin and Yang inside Tai Ji Quan, you would have missed the essence of Tai Ji Quan. For example, if you think that Tai Ji Quan is only soft and never hard, and it embodies only Yin and never Yang—you would probably be doing a Tai Ji dance rather than Tai ji Quan. If you perform only the external form of Tai Ji Quan without appreciating its inner aspects of energy flow and mind calming—performing only Yang Pole and missing Yin Pole—you would practice a physical exercise rather than an internal art. In "The Great Appendix" to the *I Ching*, Confucius said, "The combination of Yin and Yang creates Tao." It talks about the relationship among the three—Tai Ji, Yin-Yang and Tao. Everything in the nature has two parts containing the same relationship as the two poles. Therefore, Tai Ji Quan teaches people to follow the rules of nature and to combine their bodies and their thoughts with our nature, which expresses the spirit of Taoism. (229 words)

Exercises 2

Task 1 Listening Comprehension
1. A   2. D   3. C   4. A   5. A

Task 2 Spot Dictation
1. nurtured   2. famous for   3. flavor   4. relics   5. originated in
6. prosperity   7. acquired   8. preserved   9. apart from   10. constitutes

Task 3 Short Answer Questions
1. Beijing Opera synthesizes music, drama, dancing, and acrobatics in it.
2. There is very distinct Ming Dynasty influence on Beijing Opera costumes.

3. Facial masks use different colors as important ways to portray status of different characters.

4. Because there located all kinds of famous shops.

5. Because it was the leading birthplace of Beijing Opera and Xuannan Culture.

Task 4 Translation

Dashilar is famous for all kinds of stores with an antique flavor. The average customer flow reaches approximately 150—160 thousand, and it increases to more than 200 thousand on weekends and in holidays. Although this commercial street has a history of more than 580 years, most of the ancient architectures are well preserved and many famous old shops and time-honored brands in old Beijing still provide good products. The combination of royal culture and folk culture makes Dashilar a place with profound cultural foundation and dignified historical atmosphere.